LIVES&
LEGACIES

Rumi

ALSO IN THE LIVES & LEGACIES SERIES:

DIETRICH BONHOFFER by Christian Feldman

DUKE ELLINGTON by Janna Tull Steed

FRANTZ FANON by Patrick Ehlen

JOAN OF ARC by Siobhan Nash-Marshall

FRIDA KAHLO by Jack Rummel

ROBERT F. KENNEDY by Konstantin Sidorenko

JACK KEROUAC by Ken Caffrey Jr.

MAIMONIDES by Ilil Arbel

MARY QUEEN OF SCOTS by Carol Schaefer

POPE JOHN XXIII by Christian Feldman

HENRY OSSAWA TANNER by Marcus Bruce

SERIES EDITOR: BARBARA LEAH ELLIS

LESLIE WINES

Rumi

A Spiritual Biography

A Crossroad 8th Avenue Book
The Crossroad Publishing Company
New York

The Crossroad Publishing Company
481 Eighth Avenue, Suite 1550
New York, NY 10001

First published in 2000 by The Crossroad Publishing Company

LIBRARY OF CONGRESS CATALOGING-IN-PUBLICATION DATA
Wines, Leslie.
Rumi: a spiritual biography / by Leslie Wines.
p. cm. – (Lives & Legacies)
Includes bibliographical references and index.
ISBN 0-8245-2352-0
1. Jalal al-Din Rumi, Maulana, 1207-1273. 2. Mevleviyah
members—Biography. 3. Sufis—Biography.
4. Poets, Persian—Biography. I. Title.
BP189.7.M42 W56 2000
297.4'092—dc21
[B]   00-011300

Printed in the United States of America
Set in Janson
Designed and produced by SCRIBES Editorial
Cover design by Kaeser and Wilson Design Ltd.

1 2 3 4 5 6 7 8 9 10 03 02 01 00 00

to my parents

CONTENTS

Rumi

Rumi and one of his young disciples, Hosam al-Din Chelebi.
(Pierpont Morgan Library/Art Resources)

1

The Poet of Love and Tumult

> The meaning of poetry has no sureness of direction;
> it is like the sling, it is not under control.
>
> —*Jalalu'ddin Rumi*

JALALU'DDIN RUMI, THE THIRTEENTH-CENTURY Persian lawyer-divine and Sufi, widely considered literature's greatest mystical poet, understood very well the uncontrollable and idiosyncratic impact of poetry. Yet one wonders if even he, for all his intuitive grasp of language, humanity and the cosmos foresaw the deep and diverse influence his own work would have on readers throughout the world seven centuries after his death—or the myriad meanings enthusiasts would draw from his sprawling and contradictory poems.

In the Islamic world today, Rumi is read for much the same reasons he was revered during his life: for his excellence as a poet; for his rare ability to empathize with humans, animals and plants; for his personal refinement; and, above all else, for his flawless moral center and ability to direct others towards good conduct and union with Allah.

Rumi's work also has been read in the West for centuries and there have been informed references to him in the work of Ralph Waldo Emerson and Georg Wilhelm Friedrich Hegel and many other eminent writers. But in recent years the popularity of his work in the West has increased to a surprising extent: according to the *Christian Science Monitor*, Rumi ranked as America's best-selling poet in 1997. His biography, or at least the highlights of his difficult but victorious life, should prove as inspiring as his poetry to his diverse and growing readership.

The key events of Rumi's life—or those that appear to have shaped his poetry to a great extent—seem to have been his insecure childhood spent with his family roaming between countries at the time of the Mongol invasion; his close relationship with his father, the mystic Baha al-Din; his great popularity as an Islamic professor; and his unusually intense spiritual and emotional love for the dervish Shams al-Din of Tabriz.

Many Western readers prize his work less as a moral lodestar and resource for merging with the Absolute, and more as a vehicle for illuminating our own highly secular age. Although, to be sure, these readers also are drawn to the ecstatic and transcendental qualities of the great mystic's work. Western admirers tend to extract Rumi from his historical context and embrace him as one of their own. Not a few have seized on his poetry as a springboard for their own creative expressions, including New York clothes designer Donna Karan, who in 1998 unveiled her spring line of fashions while musical interpretations of Rumi's work by the health writer Deepak Chopra played in the background. Composers Philip Glass and Robert Wilson have written "Monsters of Grace," an operatic extravaganza that can be enjoyed with three-dimensional viewing glasses and a libretto of one hundred and fourteen Rumi poems interpreted by American poet Coleman Barks.

Quick-thinking American entrepreneurs seem to devise new means to capitalize on Rumi's soaring popularity nearly every month. Recently, several versions of "Rumi cards," a new method of fortune-telling, combining snippets of the poet's work and aspects of the Tarot, have appeared in U.S. bookstores. And, for those who peruse the World Wide Web, it is possible to dial up "rumi.com" and be informed that, "In the name of God, Most Gracious, Most Merciful, Jalalu'ddin Rumi.com is coming soon."

Commercialism aside, the differences between the Islamic and Western view of Rumi probably become most apparent when exploring the subject of love, a central preoccupation of the poet's work. Western readers have been captivated by Rumi's frequent and masterful use of romantic imagery, which, coupled with the medieval lack of prudery have caused some to regard him chiefly as a love poet. Many are fascinated with Rumi's mystic identification and all-encompassing spiritual love for his mentor Shams al-Din of Tabriz. Some construe this relationship as a conventional love affair, given Rumi's frequent declarations of his overwhelming longing for Shams after Shams' mysterious departure. Indeed, in 1998, the gay magazine *The Advocate* published a piece in which it was argued that Islamic scholars have obscured a likely gay relationship between the poet and Shams. Other Western readers are charmed by the lack of priggishness and the nearly Chaucerian quality contained in some of Rumi's depictions of heterosexual couplings.

Yet Islamic scholars consistently have interpreted the relationship between Rumi and Shams as an example of the Sufi call to open one's heart to another human, in order to open one's heart to God. At the same time, Rumi's frequent use of ardent, earthy imagery to describe his affinity with his beloved Shams also is in keeping with the conventions of Persian love poetry, which sometimes used sexual imagery to depict platonic love between men.

Similarly, anecdotes of sexual love are not necessarily viewed as mindless endorsements of licentiousness by Islamic readers, but sometimes as ironic and cautionary commentaries on human nature. And in other ways, Islamic readers enjoy a very different Rumi. To the Islamic mind, there are no necessary divisions between the secular and spiritual realms, or between man and

God. Rumi's bawdiest jokes, his most erotically-charged images, his cosmopolitan grasp of cultures and religions outside his own, and his fluent knowledge of law, history, literature and nature are not viewed as ends in themselves: they are only devices for expediting readers' connection with Allah and the unseen world. For all the dazzling breadth and variety of the *Mathnawi*, Rumi's six-volume masterpiece, the work also may be said to have had only a single purpose: communion with the Absolute.

For Islamic readers, Rumi remains an important commentator on the Koran and a brilliant exponent of Sufi philosophy, the strain of Islam that stresses direct and ecstatic communion with Allah over Aristotelian questioning. Rumi, who was strictly educated in religious law and philosophy, is viewed in the Islamic world as a spiritual descendant of two other great Sufi writers, Sana'i and Attar. He shared with those two writers the goal of eliminating corruption from religious practice and institutions. He also is widely seen as the vindicator of his father, Baha al-Din, an Islamic preacher whose metaphysical and mystical leanings often were greeted with skepticism because of a prevailing bias towards Aristotelian inquiry in his native Khorosan, today known as Afghanistan.

In Turkey today, Rumi is revered by many as the founder of the Mevlevi Order, which is associated with the colorful "whirling dervishes," the Sufis who twirl themselves into joyful merger with the Absolute. Indeed, Rumi himself helped make popular the once questionable practice of this mystic dance by twirling, first in the marketplace, and later, to the astonishment of many, at a funeral for a beloved friend. Iran, which has assumed the role of the preserver of Persian culture, has in recent years offered its respects to the poet through an abundant outpouring of new scholarly essays.

So, WHY ARE there so many views of Rumi, and so many ways to read him? How can so many types of contemporary readers connect so intimately, and apparently quite sincerely, with this long-dead medieval writer?

In his work, Rumi tells us over and over that he is attempting to put into language the nature and significance of the invisible universe, a task he freely admits can only be achieved in part. In "The Story of Solomon and the Hoopoe," Rumi writes: "Do thou hear the name of every thing from the knower? Hear the inmost meaning of the mystery of He That Taught the Names. With us, the name of every thing is its outward appearance, with the Creator, the name of every thing is its inward reality."[1]

The best explanation for Rumi's popularity may simply be that he was a very wonderful poet—uniquely capable of transcending "outward appearances" and conjuring up the mystical "inward reality," yet entirely realistic and modest about the limitations of his words—and there are very few such writers in the world. It also must be remembered that the *Mathnawi*, Rumi's longest work, is a Persian classic and by itself would ensure his literary immortality.

Another part of Rumi's very broad appeal may derive from his genuinely cosmopolitan character; if many types of people today feel linked to Rumi, it may be because in his lifetime he enjoyed unusually good relations with diverse groups. Born in or near Balkh in the province of Khorosan, in what is now Afghanistan—an area with Buddhist, Islamic, Christian, Zoroastrian and Jewish traditions—Rumi apparently was familiar with all those religions and often friendly with their practitioners. After the death of his first wife, an Islamic woman, Rumi chose as his second wife a woman many people believed to be of Christian origin. This second marriage took place, somewhat remarkably, at the time of the Crusades, when large portions of the Christian and Islamic worlds were preoccupied with conquering each other. The hagiographers tell us that there was no more beautiful tribute to Rumi's universality than his funeral, a forty-day marathon of grieving attended by distraught, weeping Muslims, Christians, Jews, Greeks, Arabs and Persians.

Then again, the loose, rambling structure of Rumi's work—especially the *Mathnawi,* which is full of free associations and abrupt changes of topic—makes for a grab-bag style of poetry, capable of engaging many different people because it contains a wealth of topics. Some of the slightly chaotic quality of Rumi's works may be attributed partly to the fact that he did not write it down himself. Rather, he dictated his poems and musings to scribes who followed him about, attempting to keep up with his fast-paced mind. The scholar Annemarie Schimmel in the *Triumphal Sun* tells us something about the conditions under which Rumi's mysterious changeable poetry was produced:

> The looseness of the *Mathnawi,* which most readers find difficult to appreciate, is reminiscent of the form of mystical sessions [which Rumi held with his disciples]; the master gives some advice or expresses an opinion; some visitor or disciple may utter a word; he takes it up, spins a new tale out of it, is caught by some verbal association— very common in the Islamic languages with their almost infinite possibilities of developing different meanings from one Arabic root—then, he may become enraptured and recite some verses, and thus the evening passes in an enchanted atmosphere; but it would be difficult to remember the wonderful stories and points the next day in any logical sequence.[2]

As for Western readers, there is another important reason for Rumi's surprisingly strong appeal today: his ability to evoke ecstasy from the plain facts of nature and everyday life. One often gets the sense that merely to draw breath, or catch sight of another crea-ture, are immensely pleasurable events. Many of Rumi's poems convey feelings of great joy in being able to play any sort of role at all in the natural order. And such confident expressions of belong-ing and pleasure are too rare in the technologically sophisticated, but socially fragmented modern world. Consider this translation of a section of the *Mathnawi*, by Jonathan Star:

> My soul wants to fly away when your presence calls it so sweetly.
> My soul wants to take flight, when you whisper, "Arise."
> A fish wants to dive from dry land into the ocean, when it hears the drum beating "Return."
> A Sufi, shimmering with light, wants to dance like a sunbeam when darkness summons him.[3]

In short, Rumi's work responds to an increasing need many of us have for an instinctive and mystical response to the ordinary events of life, and for a more joyful daily existence. For, although Rumi's work is peppered throughout with biting social commen-tary, cynicism and a mordant wit, the overall effect of reading his poetry is very encouraging, as if some small portion of his vast inner state has been transferred to the reader. Moreover, Rumi was indeed a very great love poet—whether his work is inter-preted in an earthy, secular context, or within a strictly spiritual framework. His aching longing for Shams and his poetical dis-sections of the many states of love provide readers with a vocab-ulary for exploring the wide array of their own emotional and spiritual states. The love documented by Rumi is very complex, a privilege and a torment, laced with many shades of sadness and joy and bewilderment. There is little sentimentality for its own sake in Rumi's work; his meditations on love often shed light upon its turbulent and unsettling aspects, while also illuminating its transformational potential. In the *Divan-e*, Rumi writes:

You are in love with me, I shall make you perplexed.
Do not build much, for I intend to have you in ruins.
If you build two hundred houses in a manner that the bees do;
I shall make you as homeless as a fly.
If you are the mount Qaf in stability.
I shall make you whirl like a millstone.[4]

These sorts of meditations on love probably are eagerly read today by many in the West, not just for their superb imagery, but because readers today desperately want to probe love more fully and participate in its most mysterious and inchoate aspects. Yet we find ourselves in a culture that sometimes approaches love as a dull series of kitschy moments, the better to patronize it.

Rumi's contemporary relevance can also be found in the frequently severe and unsettling circumstances of his life. Like many people in both the Islamic and Western worlds today, Rumi lived through extraordinary social and political tumult. It appears that the poet was able to convey the chaotic nature of poetry and life very convincingly because his own life was placed in uncertainty and danger on many occasions, during both his childhood and his adult years, sometimes due to political instability, and other times due to profound inner change. Many modern readers, finding themselves in tumultuous conditions, take comfort in the way the poet transcended and triumphed over harrowing circumstances.

THE AREA IN WHICH RUMI'S family lived during his early childhood was under threat of the Mongol invasion. There are many indications that the terror unleashed in the Islamic world by the

Mongols was the principal reason his family left its native Khorosan while Rumi was still a young child. However, a few texts suggest that Rumi's father decided to leave because he did not enjoy the level of influence he felt he deserved as a distinguished Islamic thinker.

In either case, Rumi, perhaps at the tender age of ten or twelve, along with many of his relatives, fled Khorosan, an area in which the family had lived for generations. They began an approximately ten-year, fifteen hundred-mile trek and eventually reestablished themselves in Konya in Asiatic Anatolia, or modern Turkey. Along the way, young Rumi lost his mother, one of his father's four wives, and most probably experienced numerous other sorrows and deprivations. Scholars have suggested that Rumi's imperturbable inner state and his mystic sensibility were cultivated in large part as a defense against the transience, loss and terror he endured during his childhood.

After settling in Konya, Rumi apparently had a fairly stable early adulthood, becoming his father's intellectual successor and traveling to meet other scholars. Initially, he settled into the fairly conventional life of an Islamic lawyer-divine and scholar and enjoyed great prestige in Konya. Yet he was to purposefully rattle his own secure existence at the age of thirty-seven when he suddenly formed his extraordinary mystical friendship with the eccentric dervish Shams al-Din of Tabriz. After encountering Shams, Rumi's life changed as much as it had when he had left Khorosan as a child. As the literary critic Fatemeh Keshavarz so aptly puts it: "Shams awakened in Rumi the wayfarer who had to free himself of rational and speculative knowledge to seek new horizons." If encountering Shams was an experience of freedom and enlightenment for Rumi, losing the dervish was one of great loss and heartbreak, intensified by the possibility that Shams was murdered by one of Rumi's own sons.

Rumi's fascinating and itinerant, if sometimes harrowing childhood, as well as his watershed encounter with his mystical Beloved Shams, and his subsequent creation of brilliant lyrics, are stories which can be grasped by both medieval and modern people. These stories, as much as Rumi's poetry, resound with people today caught up in social upheaval beyond their control, as well as those who deliberately unravel their own conventional security in search of more meaningful lives.

Exterior. Selimye Camii, Kony, Turkey.
(Vanni/Art Resource, NY)

2

A Harsh Childhood of Few Facts

It is meet that Heaven should rain tears of blood on earth
At the destruction that has befallen.
—from Sa'di's elegy on the sack of Baghdad

RUMI WAS PROBABLY ONLY ABOUT five years old in 1212 when the ruthless conquering Khwarazmshah sacked the Khorosan city of Samarqand, in present-day Afghanistan, where the future poet lived with his family. Yet years later he provided this clear recollection of the Khwarazmshah's assault on the ruler of Samarqand, Qarakhanid Osman:

We were in Samarqand, and the Khwarazmshah had laid siege to Samarqand and deployed his army to the attack. In that quarter dwelt an exceedingly beautiful girl, so lovely that there was none the match of her in all the city. I heard her saying, "Oh God, how canst Thou hold it allowable to deliver me into the hands of evildoers?"[1]

In this apparently true anecdote the young woman was miraculously spared from rape and assault, although most other women of the city, including her own servants, were attacked brutally. Many men also were killed by the invaders. Rumi concludes that she was protected from harm by the strength and sincerity of her prayers. He was to remember the fates of many of the other less fortunate Samarqand residents throughout his life, a tragic memory that reveals much about the political terror that persisted throughout Rumi's childhood.

In a sense, it is difficult to connect this picture of a very young boy trapped in a bloody siege, as his town's inhabitants prayed desperately for survival, with the subsequent image many of us hold today of the adult Rumi, the sublime poet. But, judging by his own accounts, Rumi's childhood indeed was marked at many points by social and political upheaval and sometimes by brushes with violence. During the early thirteenth century, the major cities of eastern Khorosan were frequently trapped in violent power shifts between members of the Ghurid, Khwarezmian and Qarakhanid clans. Rumi later described the animalistic social order under the Khwarazmshah in the *Divan-e*, saying, "The word is an arrow, and the tongue is the bow of the Khwarezmians." The already grim state of affairs in eastern Khorosan was to deteriorate into complete devastation when the Mongol assault on the region began in earnest around 1220.

The insecurity of Rumi's early years was intensified by the uneven fortunes of his father, the lawyer-divine and preacher Baha al-Din. In addition, the family eventually decided to abandon Khorosan for distant Konya in Anatolia, present-day Turkey, while Rumi was still a child, completely dismantling the foundations of his early life. From one perspective, Rumi's childhood was a long series of adverse events. Yet some scholars believe the instability of Rumi's early life helped develop him as a mystic and poet, forcing him to cultivate his rich inner life as a defense against a volatile and heartless world. The Islamic scholar Annemarie Schimmel has noted the surprising way in which culture and mysticism flourished amid political terror throughout thirteenth-century Islamic society:

The Siege of Konya, showing salt coming out of the dome
over the tomb of Rumi, founder of the
"Order of the Dancing Dervishes." (c. 1594)
(Pierpont Morgan Library/Art Resources, NY)

Strangely enough this period of the most terrible political disaster was, at the same time, a period of highest religious and mystical activity. It seems as though the complete darkness on the worldly plane was counteracted by a hitherto unknown brightness on the spiritual plane.[2]

Rumi's tale about the siege of Samarqand also underscores the fact that he and many of his contemporaries found a strong defense against the harsh realities of medieval life in their religious convictions. It's telling that, in this instance, Rumi, who only intermittently provided details of his life story in his voluminous writings, recollected very clearly the story of the beautiful girl's unlikely deliverance. He states that he believes that this marvel was not an accident, but rather the inevitable result of her strong Islamic faith and prayer.

The young Rumi's careful attention to the girl's prayer seems to indicate that his ability to decipher the complex workings of religious and mystical phenomenon may have been present even during his early childhood. This may not be surprising, given that his father Baha al-Din, whom Rumi was to eventually succeed, was learned in Islamic law and also pursued mysticism, and that the household was apparently permeated with religiosity.

Actually, we don't know if Rumi was really about five years old at the time of the Khwarazmshah's siege of Samarqand, which later was nearly demolished by the subsequent invasion of the Mongol army. In fact, it is difficult to establish most of the specifics of Rumi's life with any degree of certainty. The basic facts of Rumi's extraordinary life often prove even more elusive than the meanings of his poetry.

Through his writings, we learn much about Rumi's religious ideas and mystical interests, and something about some of the

Autonomous Sphere of Symbols
Light the Way

Mystical dreams play a special role in Sufism. The function of these dreams is to illuminate the world of the imagination, an autonomous sphere of symbols and representations that is viewed as real, but as existing beyond the tangible, material universe. In Sufism, the world of the imagination is thought to exist in a state of suspension apart from physical reality. This dominion is much like an image reflected in a mirror which can be viewed three-dimensionally, although the image itself is not a three-dimensional object.

Sufis believe that only the dreams of the Prophet Mohammad were actual prophecies. They regard their own dreams as positive indications from the imaginative realm that they are on the road to sainthood. In their prayers Sufi mystics often request to be given a dream-world spiritual chaperon to help lead them into the "way of the return." Sometimes these spirit-world aides are given somewhat arcane names like "Perfect Nature" and "Invisible Guide."

In some cases, Sufis who cannot find a suitable living master, or prefer not to do so, claim that they receive their instruction in a dream from a deceased master who functions as an "invisible guide." This appears to have been the case with Attar, whom Rumi believed had been initiated in his dreams by the ghost of the controversial mystic Mansur al-Hallaj.

An early thirteenth-century mystic named Najmoddin Kobra once described a dream in which his own face suddenly began to emit light, as if flashing beams were radiating from his face. He then saw a second face, also with flashing lights, encountering his face. In Sufi terms, this second face was a suprasensory guide, a response to his prayer for a Friend to lead him on a spiritual path. Behind the second face was a turning, vibrating sun, which was intensifying the vibrant light of the dream. The dreamer perceived that the second face was actually another manifestation of his face, and that the sun was the essence of his spirit. This sun entered his entire body, which began to emit its own brilliant rays. The dreamer then described a process in which he began to perceive not merely with his sense organs, but with his entire body.

In the sixteenth century, a Sufi named Shams ud-Din Lahiji described a dream in which he perceived that the universe itself is made up of light. In this dream, every atom in the universe rose up and declared "I am the truth!" The Sufi said he then had an intense desire to fly through the air, but he realized that a log of wood was placed across his feet, preventing him from taking flight. He violently thrust the log off his feet, and journeyed through the air until he arrived at a heavenly body. Perceiving that the moon had split into two parts he proceeded to fly through the space between the moon, back to his home on earth. He then woke up.

arkable scholars and dervishes who influenced him. But
re is little of the standard biographical facts expected by modern readers. Much of this data has been lost in the vapors of time in large part because Rumi's preoccupation was with mystical truths, not mundane facts. His writings are full of vitality and strange wisdom, but short on particulars.

In addition, his hagiographers, including those who knew Rumi during his life and those who lived afterward, aren't always reliable in their accounts. Eager to establish his genius and his sanctity, they often resorted to exaggerations and fantastical episodes to enhance his legend. These hagiographers are an interesting story unto themselves, given that all were quite lively writers, but none left a completely trustworthy account of the poet's life. Reading their texts is both enjoyable and annoying because these writings at times can be more distracting than illuminating. In their imaginative efforts to burnish Rumi's image, his disciple biographers in some cases made facts and events that were already shadowy even more confusing.

RUMI'S PRINCIPAL BIOGRAPHER in his lifetime was his favorite son and eventual successor as the head of the Mevlevi Order, Sultan Valad. The son turned his chronicling of his father's life and related events into his principal task in life. Yet Sultan Valad's accounts do not always contain the ring of truth, possibly because he is conveying the history of a family of which he is part, and few people can write with complete clarity and objectivity about their own families. In addition, his memory appears clouded at times when he relates events that happened during his early childhood, while his accounts of circumstances before his birth sometimes appear to be based on slightly dusty second-hand family lore.

Moreover, Sultan Valad, in keeping with Sufi tradition, wrote in verse and this sort of literary constraint generally places limits on how much of a story may be rendered. By the time Sultan Valad produced his history of his family and his order, Persian literature had developed entrenched conventions about how to describe a great Sufi mystic, a restriction, which sometimes caused Sultan Valad and subsequent hagiographers to favor stock clichés about religious piety over realistic histories.

Another important hagiographer was Faridun Sepahsalar, a rough contemporary of Sultan Valad who was acquainted with Rumi's son and other family members. Sepahsalar's work is the second-oldest source of biographical information about Rumi. According to his own histories, which were completed long after Rumi's death around 1315, Sepahsalar studied under Rumi. His descriptions of Rumi's life and times at points convey great sincerity and are quite believable. Yet at other times there is a troublingly naïve edge, due perhaps to Sepahsalar's devotion to the poet and his family and the Mevlevi Order, all of which he, too, wished to depict in a glowing light.

After Sepahsalar, the next important hagiographer was Shams al-Din Ahmad al-Aflaki, who lived and worked in the Mevlevi Order's lodge and completed his work sometime after 1350. Aflaki did not meet Rumi in person, but he mentions interviews with the wife of Sultan Valad. His writing is clever and potent, but so fanciful as to be perhaps the most unbelievable of all the hagiographers. A modern reader could be forgiven for wondering if, in our time, Aflaki wouldn't have turned to science fiction.

Other Rumi medieval hagiographers of interest include Dowlatshah, a fifteenth-century writer who worked only from secondary sources and Jami Abd al-Rahman, who also lived about two hundred years after the poet's death. A number of excellent modern historians, including Abdulbaki Golpinarli, Afzal Iqbal, Franklin Lewis and Annemarie Schimmel have waded carefully through the various accounts of the hagiographers, without reaching consensus on a number of key historical points.

As mentioned, even Rumi's birth date is hard to establish with complete certainty. Generally it is given as September 30, 1207, but there are several good reasons to think it could have been earlier. For instance, his recollection of the sacking of Samarqand may be a bit too clear if he was then a five-year-old child, even a very precocious one; although this story could be the result of having heard the anecdote retold to him many times by family members. There is also the fact that by most accounts Baha al-Din was near sixty at the time of Rumi's birth and past seventy when he undertook, along with many members of his family, the roughly fifteen hundred-mile trip to Anatolia. Some observers consider it more likely that Baha al-Din, was younger when Rumi was born and when the family was uprooted, a circumstance which most likely would place both Rumi's birth and the journey earlier.

Beyond doubt, the poet was born in the province of Khorosan, perhaps in the city of Balkh or maybe in the town of Vakhsh. Many historians have placed Rumi's birth in Balkh, one of the major cultural centers of Khorosan where his grandfather, Hosayn Khatibi, the father of Baha al-Din, most likely lived, and where Baha al-Din himself may have spent some years. This notion that Rumi was born in Balkh may stem from the fact that after Baha al-Din and his family arrived in Anatolia, they generally described themselves as being from Balkh. However, they may have given this location only for convenience because the city was large enough to be well known to the people of Anatolia. The scholar Franklin Lewis believes that Baha al-Din and his family lived in the smaller town of Vakhsh between 1204 and 1210, the period during which Rumi probably was born.

BAHA AL-DIN DID NOT ENJOY special status or patronage in Vakhsh, and often was held in contempt by the local inhabitants because he occupied a relatively low rank among the ulema, the class of intellectuals that provided Islamic society with legal and religious guidance. Possibly for this reason, Baha al-Din and his family moved on to Samarqand sometime between 1210 and 1212 and soon endured the siege of that city.

The family's abandonment of Khorosan altogether appears to have taken place sometime between 1219 and 1221, when Rumi probably was somewhere between twelve and fourteen years old; however, some scholars place the family's removal much earlier, while a minority believe it took place later. All these sketchy facts make it difficult to decide whether the family moved long before or shortly before the Mongol invasion.

What else can be said with certainty about Rumi's earliest childhood? His mother was named Mo'mene Khatun. Baha al-Din had at least two, and possibly three, other wives, although it is unclear if the women all were married to him at the same time. Little else can be said about Rumi's mother, except that she apparently died during the family's journey to Konya and was buried in the Anatolian town of Larende, where the family appears to have stayed for some months or possibly even years. Rumi also had a brother named Ala al-Din, who may have died during the family's period of wandering, and after whom Rumi later named one of his two sons by his first wife. Baha al-Din appears to have had at least one son and one daughter by his other wives.

There is also a charming but improbable story, told by several of Rumi's hagiographers concerning his prodigious mystical traits during early childhood. Supposedly, Rumi was asked by his playmates to jump from the terrace of one building to that of another building. Rumi's reply is said to have been that such displays are more appropriate for cats and dogs. He then invited his little friends to jump with him to visit God's dwelling in the heavens.

Despite the haziness that surrounds much of Rumi's child-

Calligraphic rendering of the phrase "In the name of
the benevolent and forgiving God." (Islamic)
(Snark/Art Resource, NY)

hood and subsequent biographical data, an intriguing, if incomplete, life story emerges. Here and there Rumi gives us a vivid description of an actual event, such as the sack of Samarqand; but the poet certainly left us with no systematic set of images of his life. The basic verifiable components of Rumi's life are his remarkable literary achievements, written descriptions of a few of his intriguing companions and relatives, and historical records of the violent and tumultuous era in Islamic history in which he lived. In the end, we may know just about as much as Rumi, with his aptitudes for both clarity and evasion, would have deemed we needed to know.

3

A King With No Dominion

Sometimes my heart fills with the thought that I am a king
with no dominion, a judge with no authority, a man of standing
with no position, and a wealthy man with no money.[1]

—*Baha al-Din*

IT WOULD BE IMPOSSIBLE TO UNDERSTAND Rumi's life and writing without studying the profound influence of his father. Rumi was both the son and spiritual successor of Baha al-Din, and the two men shared a deep fascination with mystical phenomena, and a rare ability to comprehend the invisible spheres. As the biographer Afzal Iqbal put it, Rumi, thanks to his father, was raised in "an atmosphere of dynamic mysticism." From Baha al-Din's diary of religious musings the *Ma'aref*, we learn that he was probably quite a good father, or, at the very least, a concerned father, who valued his children as highly as his work. Baha al-Din writes: "Every moment I hear a cry from one of the children I would sigh, thinking, 'What calamity has befallen my child now?' I would think to myself, 'If I spend my life worrying over them, I'll be ruined and if I keep to myself, will they be ruined?'"[2]

Baha al-Din's devotion to Rumi becomes especially interesting when one considers their large age difference. Baha al-Din probably was born in about 1148 and appears to have been about sixty years old at the time of Rumi's birth. He was to live until his son was about twenty-four years old, although there are indications in the *Ma'aref* that he had not expected to live so long. Yet there is every sign that throughout those last years of his life, he exerted himself, much as a younger man would, on behalf of his beloved and precocious son, whom he apparently would seat beside himself when he preached.

Baha al-Din and Rumi at many times appeared almost indistinguishable in matters of philosophy and writing. Yet their fortunes and social standings could not have been more different. Rumi by all accounts led a sort of charmed life, enjoying a first-class education, a reputation for eloquence and a large following in all classes of society, including among wealthy persons and government officials. Baha's life was far less privileged, and at many points quite unpleasant. The mystical awareness that was to win great influence for Rumi did very little to advance the standing of his father, who seemed to acquire substantial respect only during the last few years of his life, when the family had settled in Konya, long after leaving Khorosan.

The social stature of Baha al-Din's ancestors is hard to gauge. Some hagiographers fancifully traced the family's lineage to Abu Bakr, the first Caliph of Islam. But this claim probably was part of their determined aggrandizement of Rumi. Subsequent historians have found it very hard to form definite conclusions about the family's distant origins or standing, or its precise ethnic background.

A Sunni Muslim of the Hanafi rite, Baha al-Din was a Muslim preacher, like his father Hosayn Khatibi, and his paternal grandfather, Ahmad al-Khatibi. According to some historians, either the father or grandfather (most likely the grandfather) of Rumi numbered prominent people among his pupils, an indication that the teacher, too, most likely was prominent. In the *Ma'aref*, Baha al-Din writes that he delivered religious lectures and taught courses on the Koran and related religious subjects. There are

Interior. Selimye Camii, Konya, Turkey.
(Vanni/Art Resource, NY)

indications that he was not associated with a particular madrase, or Islamic law college. Not being especially exalted or in demand, he may have divided his time among various mosques.

Baha al-Din was also a lawyer-divine, one of the jurisconsultants who offered legal opinions on points of Islamic law and practice. Although fascinated by meditation and mysticism, the hard science of Islamic law offered Rumi's father and others like him, the surest means of support. The judgments of lawyer-divines generally were based on the text of the Koran and incidents from the life of the Prophet Mohammad. In Islam the Koran, which Mohammad is said to have transcribed directly from the speech of God, is seen as more than a sacred book; it is viewed as "uncreated," or identical with God.

The opinions issued by lawyer-divines were not always legally binding, but generally yielded strong social influence. However, as we shall see, Baha al-Din's legal findings sometimes were met with scorn, and did little to increase his prestige. Rumi's principal hagiographers Aflaki and Sepahsalar later went to imaginative lengths to portray Baha al-Din as a distinguished lawyer-divine with scores of disciples, and as a man whose legal opinions held great influence. But these distortions were undertaken largely to polish Rumi's legend. In truth, Baha al-Din had little prominence in his lifetime and is remembered today only because he was the father of the poet. From Baha al-Din's own writings we learn that he was ridiculed often while living in Khorosan, especially in Vakhsh where Rumi may have been born and where the family lived before moving to Samarqand. In Vakhsh Rumi's father's legal opinions were considered mediocre by many powerful people.

In the *Ma'aref*, Baha al-Din tells us that he once challenged the Qazi of Vakhsh, a senior judge of that city, on the Qazi's assertion that Baha was not well-educated enough to be a significant religious leader and jurisconsultant. According to Baha the

Qazi tried to sway other Vakhsh inhabitants from listening to Baha al-Din's views. Even the hagiographer Aflaki, who sometimes exaggerated Baha al-Din's attainments, lists a number of other prominent citizens of Vakhsh who disparaged Baha al-Din's ideas and talents.

According to the scholar Franklin Lewis, Rumi's father may have inadvertently increased the animosity toward him by sometimes signing his legal opinions with the title *Sultan al-Ulema*, or "chief of the jurisconsultants." He said he had acquired the right to use this signature, with its grandiose ring, through a dream which he said occurred to an unnamed prominent person. The person was told in his dream that Baha al-Din indeed was the Sultan al-Ulema. The Qazi of Vakhsh, who thought this title was not justified, apparently would erase it from written findings, thus compounding his ridicule of Baha al-Din. There are a few hints that there in fact may have been some deficiency in Baha al-Din's educational background; so perhaps there was some justification for disparaging his credentials for making legal findings. One suggestion of this possible educational deficiency comes from the preacher's own grandson, Sultan Valad, the son of Rumi and one of the poet's most important hagiographers.

In his writings, Sultan Valad describes the reaction of the tutor Sayyed Borhan al-Din Mohaqqeq, who had been the student of Baha al-Din and who later became the tutor of Rumi, on encountering the now orphaned Rumi after many years of separation from the family. According to Sultan Valad, Borhan found Rumi to be more knowledgeable than his father. Of course, Sultan Valad also often sought to aggrandize Rumi, so this description, too, may be exaggerated or false.

IN ADDITION TO THE condescension he endured in Vakhsh, Baha al-Din evidently also was displeased with the town's paltry cultural offerings. Unlike Balkh and Samarqand, which were cultural centers of medieval Khorosan—Vakhsh was a depressingly backward place. In the *Ma'aref*, we get a picture of him, quite typically, drawing on his vast reserve of spiritual strength to cope with the disappointments of his life. At length, Baha concludes that his earthly troubles are not ultimately significant compared to the joys of his relationship with his God. He writes:

> My heart began to wonder why Vakhsh? Others are in Samarqand or Baghdad or Balkh, in majestic cities. I'm stuck in this bare, boring and forgotten corner! [Then] God inspired me with this thought: If you are with Me and I am your companion, you will not be in any place—not Vakhsh, not Baghdad, or Samarqand.[3]

If Baha al-Din could be said to have had a complete antithesis in his approach to life and secular authorities during his years in Khorosan it would have been his contemporary, the preacher and Aristotelian thinker Fakhr al-Din Razi, considered by many to be the most influential cleric in Khorosan. Historians tell us that, thanks largely to the Khwarazmshah's patronage, Razi frequently was accompanied by a retinue of about three hundred followers. In his writings Baha al-Din sharply criticized Razi, calling him a "deviant" for pandering to wealthy and powerful people, and constantly boasting about his intellectual powers. The indignant Baha also denounced the Khwarazmshah himself as another "deviant," for contributing to the prominence of Razi.

Other writers have claimed that Razi was so arrogant as to play on the fact that his first name of Mohammad was also that of the Prophet, insinuating, perhaps, that the two occupied roughly similar spiritual stations. In the *Maqalat*, Rumi's spiritual companion Shams al-Din of Tabriz alleged that Razi had bragged obnoxiously of having read every book written after Aristotle. For his part, Razi was equally derisive of Sufism and other forms of mysticism, though it is unclear whether Baha al-Din was sufficiently prominent for Razi to bother even to attack him personally. A rational theorist, he made it clear that he regarded Sufi mysticism as both intellectually insubstantial and a form of trickery.

The writer Afzal Iqbal tells a quite funny anecdote about Razi's attempts to diminish Sufism in the eyes of the Khwarazmshah, who apparently maintained good relations with both logical philosophers and Sufis, to the consternation of Razi. According to Iqbal, a Persian historian named Tarikh-i-Wassaf recorded that it annoyed Razi greatly that the Khwarazmshah sometimes turned to the Sufis for advice. To retaliate, Razi ordered workers in the Khwarazmshah's stable to dress as Sufis and surrounded them with a crowd of people who pretended to be their followers. Razi then told the Khwarazmshah the crowd had asked to meet him, and the ruler came and politely asked for their help. Shortly afterward, Razi exposed the prank, telling the Khwarazmshah that just about anyone can pretend to be a spiritual leader, implying that the Sufis were religious fakes.

A few historians have suggested that either Razi, or Baha al-Din's bitter relationship with him, helped drive Rumi's family out of Khorosan. The problem with this theory is that Razi died well before the family made its departure for Anatolia. Nonetheless, Razi's belittling behavior made life in Khorosan difficult for the Sufis and other mystics. And the repercussions of this hostile social climate were particularly unfortunate for Baha al-Din.

In a fascinating coda, Razi, in the very final days of his life apparently had a dramatic reversal of heart and told one of his students that many of his intellectual attainments had been superficial and had brought little spiritual comfort. In the *Maqalat*, Shams al-Din of Tabriz imagines Razi at the end of his life finally realizing that, "Lifelong debate brought no profit to us, for we gathered from it only words, words."

By contrast, Baha al-Din's writings reveal that he considered himself morally upright and unable to render insincere legal views merely to flatter powerful people. He was convinced that his integrity and refusal to compromise were the reasons he was not favored by authorities. In the *Ma'aref* Baha al-Din also suggested that he may have been better off without the patronage of powerful leaders, deducing that such associations can lead to spiritual compromise. Yet his words on this subject seem poignant at times, as if he also understood all too well that his rather lowly station forced him to forgo certain worldly advantages. As he mentions in the *Ma'aref*, at times he felt like a "king with no standing," or a "man with no position." However, at such moments Baha al-Din would remind himself that thoughts of envy and greed only make one unhappy, and he would remind himself to focus on his God. According to Baha al-Din's calculations, worldly ambition was like a long and high ladder and those who ascended it would likely fall off on some middle rung.

THE RELIGIOSITY OF Baha al-Din, which in time would shape Rumi's cosmology and poetry, was not bland or sentimental: it derived from difficult and sustained meditations and efforts to transcend mundane reality. From the *Ma'aref*, we learn that he often spent long private hours traversing the universe and fusing with his God in his mind. The God of Baha al-Din does not resemble an Old Testament father figure, or most of the more modern concepts of God, but rather appears to be a vast and largely indescribable metaphysical reality unto himself.

The profound nature of Baha al-Din's religious consciousness can be glimpsed in a section of the *Ma'aref* cited by Franklin Lewis. Baha al-Din puts forth:

When my consciousness is busied with God, I move beyond the world of existence and decomposition and have my being not in space or in a place, but I wander through the world beyond modality and look. . . .

God moved me with the thought that the four walls of your body and the space that contains you are aware of you and live through you, but do not see you. Though they do not see you, neither from within or without, yet every atom of you is filled with the evidences of you.[4]

The God known to Baha al-Din, consistent with Islamic theology suffuses himself throughout the physical universe, and is present in all places at all moments. This God never wears a human face, but instead inhabits every particle visibly and invisibly, being identical with all earthly creatures, but also having transcended them. This mysterious, all-knowing God of Baha al-Din also seems to have inhabited Rumi's literary landscape and to have helped the poet to visit the intangible universe as effortlessly as he did the transient world. At times Baha al-Din's mystical experiences sound as if they took place beyond the edges of consciousness; his writings contain descriptions of witnessing pure forms and shapes come apart and reconfigure. There is a quasi-hallucinatory quality to these musings, some of which may have followed fasting and withdrawal from society. At any rate, this sort of mental journeying was also a strong part of Rumi's spiritual and poetic heritage.

Not only did Rumi derive his grasp of mysticism and metaphysics directly from his father, but his writings markedly resemble those of Baha al-Din. The writer Afzal Iqbal jokingly notes that there are enough similarities between Baha al-Din's *Ma'aref* and Rumi's *Mathnawi* to justify charges of plagiarism.

(Not that medieval Persian writers, who freely borrowed stories and images from other sources, worried much about plagiarism.) So strong, in fact, was the influence of Baha al-Din on Rumi that Shams al-Din of Tabriz, the poet's mystical companion, later forbid Rumi from reading the *Ma'aref* for fear that Rumi's individuality would not develop.

In addition to a shared love of mysticism, Rumi and his father had a joint hostility toward Aristotelian logic. This preference for mysticism over the philosophic sciences, a key component of Sufism, blemished Baha al-Din's reputation much more than it did that of Rumi. Unfortunately for Baha al-Din, logical philosophy was in vogue in Khorosan throughout most of his life there and this bias often caused people to look down on him.

Somewhat before Baha al-Din's birth in 1148 the famous Islamic philosopher Abu Hamid Muhammad al-Ghazali, the author of *The Alchemy of Happiness*, had launched a thorough study of the entire system of philosophy which had developed in the east from Greek reasoning. Al-Ghazali, who was to influence Baha al-Din and Rumi greatly, came to the conclusion that Aristotelian philosophy lacked a solid foundation. Later in life he had a mystical experience and concluded that the "Light of God" had entered him. In time he embraced the teachings of the Sufis. Baha al-Din also considered al-Ghazali's brother, Ahmad, a writer of essays on divine love, to be a sort of spiritual ancestor.

Although a profound mystic, Baha al-Din, unlike Rumi, did not embrace Sufism outright, but he did share its emphasis on direct connection with one's God, and its dislike of intellectuality for its own sake. Strictly conventional in his morality and opposed to any deviation from the Prophet Mohammad's own behavior, he had reservations about the order's perceived social laxity and its frequent willingness to engage in conduct not associated with Mohammad.

From his writings, Rumi's father emerges as a strong personality, blessed with sufficient character and spiritual depth to persevere despite often being stigmatized, and despite living in precarious times. Of his interesting but difficult life, perhaps the most intriguing question is why he left Khorosan at such a late stage. By all indications Baha al-Din was in his late sixties or early seventies when he uprooted much of his extended household, and some of his disciples, to wander through the Middle East in search of a better life.

Why did he decide to do such a thing toward the end of his life? Or, conversely, why didn't he do it much earlier? Historians have not been able to decide on a precise reason for the departure. Of course, the frequently contemptuous attitude displayed toward mysticism and Baha al-Din himself in Khorosan most certainly wearied him and could have roused thoughts about a better life elsewhere. Yet, the most frequently given explanation was that Baha al-Din and his entourage were fleeing the impending Mongol invasion. Most historians believe the family's departure took place sometime between 1216 and 1219, when Rumi was between nine and twelve years old; however, a few believe they could have left as late as 1220.

THE MONGOL INVASION overtook Balkh and other nearby Khorosan cities in 1221, and there is a small chance that the family was still there, although most historians think it had left well before then. There also is a chance that the family sensed the impending catastrophe in advance, and left ahead of it. This theory can be traced to a subsequent insinuation by Rumi's son Sultan Valad that the invasion was a sort of deserved comeuppance for the nasty treatment Baha al-Din had endured in Khorosan. It also is possible that Baha al-Din thought it best to flee Khorosan after his denunciation of the Khwarazmshah.

Afzal Iqbal notes that the hagiographers embellished the possibility of Baha al-Din's foreknowledge of the invasion with an anecdote in which he makes a theatrical and severe warning to the Khwarazmshah. Iqbal conjures up a perhaps fictitious occasion in which the preacher delivers a sermon at a great mosque with the Khwarazmshah in attendance, just before Baha al-Din left the area. In this speech Baha al-Din is supposed to have warned the Khwarazmshah about the coming of the Mongols and the subsequent destruction of many cities in Khorosan, but the arrogant prince did not believe him. It is unclear whether this dramatically appealing scene was dreamt up by the hagiographers, or whether Baha a-Din indeed foresaw the carnage and warned the city.

In later years, in the *Divan-e* Rumi referred to what seems to be a narrow miss of the invasion by the family: "When you are in Balkh, make a move towards Baghdad, oh father; So that every moment you get farther away from Merv and Herat. . . ." The sense of foreboding in this verse would suggest that the family's flight may have been prompted by the need to evade the Mongol army, and that Rumi may have spent much of his child-hood in a state of dread, preoccupied with eluding the advanc-ing Mongols. At the very least these lines would suggest that Rumi in later years reflected deeply on the route taken by his family and the fortunate manner in which the group managed to stay a few moves ahead of the Mongols. Certainly the family's timely removal from the Balkh area enabled it to avoid some of the worst carnage of the entire Mongol conquest.

On the other hand, some historians have noted that some members of Baha al-Din's extended family did not make the journey to Anatolia. They have speculated that the patriarch would have been unlikely to leave his relatives behind if he believed they were in great danger. Of course, even without foreseeing the Mongol invasion, the family could still have fled Khorosan for political reasons. After all, they had endured the frequent violent shifts of power between the various dynasties of the region—including the siege of Samarqand—and these incidents alone could have convinced them to leave.

Whether the family left Khorosan to avoid political terror, or out of disgust with the treatment of Baha al-Din, it ultimately was to find a much better way of life in Konya. By contrast to cosmopolitan Konya in Anatolia, Khorosan was a violent, backward province, and conditions there were about to worsen severely with the advent of the Mongols. Konya, with its physical beauty, greater acceptance of mysticism, and enlightened Seljuk leader, in time was to provide the family with many years of protection from the Mongols, before that region, too, succumbed to the invaders.

4

The Never-Ending Journey

How shouldst thou, O heart, which art [but] one of these hundred thousand
particulars, not be in restless movement at His decree?
Be at the disposal of the Prince, like a horse [or mule], now confined in the
stable, now going on the road.[1]

—*Jalalu'ddin Rumi*

RUMI SPENT A GOOD PART of his early life on the move, shifting
from country to country, and city to city as his family's entourage
made its way from Khorosan to Mecca, then traveled through Syria
toward Anatolia, where it was to make many stops. The group
paused often along the way, sometimes remaining briefly in a town
or city, and other times taking up a fairly long residence in places
where Baha al-Din found patrons and opportunities to preach.

Rumi was probably around twelve years old when his family
began its wanderings, and he was about twenty-two when the group
finally settled permanently in Konya. Annemarie Schimmel has
noted that this unusual nomadic childhood must have had a deep
impact on the psyche of the future poet, and may have "influenced
Maulana's [Rumi's] feeling that life, and especially spiritual life, is a
never-ending journey, a quest for the Divine Presence of which he
was constantly aware." The constant flux and the lack of external
certainties surely sharpened Rumi's awareness of the transience of
life and may have forced him to focus on absolute truths and on his
God. The need to keep moving and not throw down deep roots
must have been quite painful at times.

Moreover, the family did not completely escape the woes of political instability when it left Khorosan. Throughout the Islamic world, assorted princes had installed themselves in various cities. Some of these rulers were reasonably stable. But others encountered bloody challenges from rival dynasties, and watched as their cities plunged into intrigue and warfare. And, although the Valad family had evaded the Mongol invasion for a while by leaving Khorosan, it was to catch up with them later, although not until they had settled for good in Konya. At any rate, Rumi's life in the caravan probably was not free of serious worries.

Yet, for all its problems, this vagabond youth also provided a unique and rather privileged education, giving Rumi rare exposure to different ethnic groups and ways of life. According to some of the hagiographers' accounts, Rumi in his travels also met distinguished poets, mystics and scholars. In the *Mathnawi* Rumi would draw frequently on his cosmopolitan upbringing with vignettes drawn from many ways of life. The extremely broad-minded inclusive quality of Rumi's poetry, in which the poet seems able to enter the consciousness of a myriad of people and other creatures, probably owes much to having enjoyed a great variety of experiences at an impressionable age.

In addition, the fortunes of Baha al-Din and the entire entourage seem to have improved almost immediately after the group made its way out of Khorosan. The hagiographers offer some fetching descriptions of mighty dignitaries humbly approaching the caravan to pay their highest respects to the great Hanafi scholar Baha al-Din. Yet these passages are much too florid not to arouse suspicions. However, it does appear that many of the places the group visited had large populations of Islamic practitioners of the Hanafi rite, which would predispose people to accept Baha al-Din. It also seems that Baha al-Din did not encounter the extreme prejudice against mysticism that had made his life so difficult in Khorosan. Whatever the harsh realities of life on the road in the medieval Middle East, in some ways it may have been an improvement over Khorosan for Rumi and his family.

What route did the family take? Again we have to content ourselves with shadowy evidence and educated guesses. The hagiographer Aflaki provides the most detailed information, but his version is riddled with the sort of fantastical episodes that place all of his facts in doubt. However, it also is worth noting that Aflaki was a contemporary of Rumi's children and knew some members of the family, a fact which should bestow some credence on his accounts. The German scholar Helmut Ritter believes that before leaving Khorosan for good, Baha al-Din returned from Samarqand to Balkh. This is when he could have delivered his fateful warning about the Mongol invasion to the Khwarazmshah, if he ever delivered such a warning at all.

The hagiographers suggest that after leaving either Balkh or Samarqand, the group stopped first in Neishapour, in what is now northeastern Iran. It is here that the young Rumi by legend had an encounter with the great mystic poet Farid ud-Din Attar, the author of *The Conference of the Birds*, a classic of Persian literature and a complicated commentary on the nature of spiritual and political power.

According to the fifteenth-century hagiographer Dowlatshah, Attar perceived the young Rumi's superior intellect and spirituality almost instantly and provided him with a copy of his work *The Book of the Mysteries*. Upon catching sight of the young boy trailing his father by a few steps Attar is supposed to have exclaimed: "What an astonishing sight! There goes a river dragging a might ocean behind it!" This anecdote, and several similar ones, reveal the great relish the hagiographers took in suggesting that the young Rumi somehow possessed a preternatural charisma and that his remarkable destiny could be foretold by wise people who encountered him as a child. There are also suggestions that Attar had hoped to persuade Baha al-Din to remain in Neishapour and teach there.

Unfortunately, we cannot be sure that the two poets ever met, and it isn't even certain that the family ever passed through Neishapour. Attar is believed to have died sometime between 1193 and 1235, a period which would include that of Rumi's family's journey. Some historians have placed Attar's death in 1229, the year the Mongols sacked Neishapour. Whether the two poets met, Attar's works were to provide literary models for Rumi; there are strong echoes of *The Conference of the Birds* in the *Mathnawi*. In addition, Attar's life story provides interesting insights into the outcast status many Sufis endured in medieval Islamic society. His poetry is full of references to Sufis who suffered for their philosophy, as Attar himself was to do.

LIKE MANY SUFIS—and like many other writers of all eras and places who dare comment critically on the nature of political leaders—Attar was something of a pariah in his society. He believed that truth often exists outside human conventions, and he was quite willing to violate social mores whenever necessary to pursue his truths. His masterwork, *The Conference of the Birds*, in theory was about a search for an ideal "sheikh," or spiritual king, yet it laid out some rather subversive truths about worldly leaders, characterizing them at many points as nasty and frivolous. By legend, Attar quite late in his life was tried and convicted for heresy for some of his other poems, and had his property confiscated.

Also like other Sufis, Attar placed special emphasis on passionate love as a means and a metaphor for annihilating one's petty ego and merging with the beloved in the form of one's God. In *The Conference of the Birds*, Attar offended some religious sensibilities by making allegories between this sort of overwhelming longing and a variety of unconventional couplings, including a liaison between a princess and a slave, and a homosexual love affair. Here we find the Sufi willingness to exceed society's boundaries to establish higher truths. While this sort of taboo smashing may have been necessary for the Sufis' pursuit of truth, it also is quite easy to imagine how such a philosophy came to be seen as a threat to society.

Whether Rumi ever met Attar or not, he was deeply impressed by his work. In later years, Rumi even added his private theory to a fascinating Sufi controversy surrounding the identity of the sheikh, or mystical teacher, of Attar. Attar, in his writings had not left a clear indication of whom his mentor was, and other Sufis had provided various guesses. Rumi's theory was that Attar did not have a living teacher, but had been taught during his dreams by the spirit of Mansur al-Hallaj, a Sufi martyr who had been executed in Baghdad in the tenth century.

In his writings the unconventional Attar displays great sympathy for al-Hallaj, and another Sufi martyr, Bistami, also known as Bayazid. Two of the most unorthodox and controversial figures in all of Sufism; these men aroused passionate responses in other Sufis, some of whom revered them and some of whom viewed them as heretics.

Not only was al-Hallaj hated by the authorities, many fellow Sufis disapproved of him because he had violated the Sufi tradition of secrecy by openly proclaiming some of Sufism's mystical doctrines. His habit of proclaiming himself 'the Truth,' or even 'God,' solidified his reputation as an intolerable heretic; however, he most likely meant only to assert that he had forfeited his individual ego and had merged with his God. In the end al-Hallaj, who also was to have a strong spiritual influence on Rumi, was put in jail for eight years before being tried and found guilty of heresy. He was then put to death in the most viscious manner imaginable: he was flogged, decapitated, and set on fire; his ashes were then scattered in the Tigris River. His death was widely viewed as a warning to all Sufis.

The other Sufi martyr celebrated by Attar, Bistami, was to have a strong influence on Rumi too. He fared slightly better than al-Hallaj, yet Bistami's life was another cautionary tale about the social perils entailed in practicing Sufism. Although widely despised, he managed to escape execution by pretending to be insane. Bistami also at times could not resist proclaiming himself the 'Absolute.' At one point, he announced he had a vision of the throne of God, and had seen himself seated in it.

As WE CAN SEE from the fates of Attar, al-Hallaj and Bistami, Sufism was often a very dangerous philosophy to espouse in medieval Islamic society. Part of the perceived dangerousness of Sufism stemmed from the apparent vagueness of its doctrines. Sufism can be hard to define beyond noting that Sufis believe that only God exists, and that everything else is an emanation of Him. Sufism, which was practiced in various forms from India to Spain in medieval times, was interpreted somewhat differently in each of the Islamic states. In some instances, Sufis also have held close various secret tenets. Sometimes Sufi adepts would explain such secret tenets aloud to their disciples, but more frequently they would transmit their philosophy wordlessly, a practice that made Sufism seem murky and questionable to outsiders. In addition, the mystic principles of Sufism were thought to be potentially dangerous to those who encountered them without appropriate preparation.

In Sufism, Islam ranks as the highest religion, but religion itself is a mere mechanism to enable people to reach the perceived higher truth of God Himself. This perception of Islam—as a means to a higher end—also was deemed as heretical by those who viewed Islam as supreme unto itself.

Moreover, the Sufis were dogged by rumors of hashish use and offbeat sexual practices involving beautiful youths in their lodges. It is difficult to establish how widespread this behavior actually was. However, it occurred often enough that Rumi, who disapproved of sexual relations with young boys, bothered to address the issue with several ironic and instructive allegories in the *Mathnawi*. Rumi's mystical companion Shams al-Din of Tabriz, aware of the proclivities of some Sufis, was to caution Rumi's second son, Sultan Valad, to avoid hashish and sex with boys.

Rumi's own relationship to the controversial nature of Sufism was itself quite fascinating, as was his relationship to the whole of society. The son of a sometimes unpopular, morally uncompromising preacher, Rumi throughout his life demonstrated great sympathy with offbeat philosophies and downtrodden and unconventional individuals. He also had an ironic understanding of the corrupting influence of power and did not go out of his way to cultivate friendships with powerful people. Yet throughout his life he was to remain extraordinarily popular with persons at all levels of society, seemingly without contriving to do so. Quite oddly, given the intense controversy generated by Sufism in medieval Islamic society, Rumi, possibly the most prominent Sufi of his time, was protected from the extremes of venom, which led to the ostracism of some Sufis and the martyrdom of others.

Rumi did not become associated strongly with Sufism until he was in his middle years, and some of his practices, such as listening to music and twirling in public in Konya, came in for harsh criticism. Yet throughout his life, he remained the darling of his disciples, and a favorite of authorities, protected, perhaps, by nothing other than his impeccable theological credentials and the sheer force of his apparently extraordinary charm.

WHETHER THE FAMILY EVER visited Attar in Neishapour or not—it appears to have stopped in Baghdad fairly early in its travels. The ever-imaginative Aflaki provides an all-too-rich description of the group's arrival in the great city. As Aflaki tells it, the Caliph himself was consumed with curiosity about the approaching caravan and desperate to learn who was in it. He called for his sheikh, Shehab al-Din Omar Sohravardi, to identify the party. Sohravardi instantly divined from the Caliph's description that the caravan could contain none other than the great scholar himself, Baha al-Din. Accompanied by other notables of Baghdad, Sohravardi ran out to greet the group.

Aflaki then describes the uncompromising Baha al-Din once more displaying his vast contempt for morally compromised political leaders by refusing to meet the Caliph. Unperturbed and in dire need of Baha al-Din's instruction, the Caliph nonetheless allows him to preach a sermon at an important mosque. During his sermon, Baha al-Din denounces the Caliph for not following the Prophet Mohammad, and makes a new warning about the impending Mongol invasion.

The hagiographer Sepahsalar also maintained that the family visited Baghdad and records that they remained there for one month. According to Aflaki, the family intended to stay in Baghdad much longer; however, Baha al-Din decided to take his family on a pilgrimage to Mecca. The sources indicate that in Mecca Baha al-Din performed the hajj, or full pilgrimage ritual. It's unclear how long the family remained in Mecca or where they went next. Some sources suggest the family traveled from Mecca to Aleppo. If they did visit Aleppo during these years, they may have witnessed another violent siege. Around 1217–1218 Seljuk sultans attacked Aleppo, which had been under the control of Ayyubid princes; the attack was repelled.

Aflaki states that the family traveled to Malatya after leaving Damascus and that Baha al-Din received, but turned down, an offer to teach there. If this account is true, his decision was vindicated in time when his old nemesis, the Khorosan Khwarazmshah, entered an alliance with al-Mozzam, the ruler of Damascus. Then, according to Aflaki, the family left Malatya around 1217, and made its way to a small Anatolian city called Aqshahr. (The orthodox Baha al-Din supposedly refused to take up residence in the nearby larger and more famous city of Erzincan because he disapproved of its large population of wine-imbibing Armenians.) While in Aqshahr, Baha al-Din benefited from the patronage of a princess named Esmati Khatun. The princess and her husband became disciples of Baha al-Din and cared for his entourage. It is unclear how long the group remained in this small city.

The group seems to have moved next to Larende, an Anatolian city populated by mainly Christians but ruled by the Seljuks. The entourage may have arrived around 1221, because there are indications that while living there Rumi turned seventeen, the age of majority in his era. At seventeen Rumi was married to Gowhar Khatun, a member of the entourage who also had traveled with the family from Samarqand. Quite possibly, Gowhar Khatun and Rumi were engaged by their parents during childhood. Gowhar Khatun's mother was one of Baha al-Din's leading disciples and the patriarch may have wished to unite his disciples through marriage.

Rumi's life was to change in other significant ways in Larende, for it is there that his mother died and was buried. His brother Ala al-Din also may have died in Larende, although that death may have occurred earlier. And it is in Larende, where Rumi's two children Ala al-Din, named for his late brother, and Sultan Valad, who came to be the poet's favorite child, were born. Possibly remaining in Larende as late as 1228, the group arrived in Konya in 1229 when Rumi by most calculations was twenty-two years old. In time the beautiful little city's reputation was to become intertwined with that of Rumi.

Exterior. Selimye Camii, Konya, Turkey.
(Vanni/Art Resource, NY)

5

Konya, At Long Last

When has anyone, even from Adam till now,
had a [melodious] voice like an organ,
Which at every preaching causes [people] to die?
His beautiful voice made two hundred human beings non-existent.[1]

—*Jalalu'ddin Rumi*

THE VALAD FAMILY FINALLY SETTLED in Konya sometime around 1228–1229, about a decade after beginning its wanderings. Rumi, who had been about ten or twelve when the caravan left Khorosan, was now in his early twenties, married and the father of two sons. The family's adopted city was to prove hospitable to Baha al-Din. Unlike Khorosan, Konya and other Anatolian cities, then under Seljuk rule, were quite receptive to mysticism. Under the Seljuks, the spread of Islam was linked strongly to mysticism.

The beautiful city of Konya was to provide an almost perfect backdrop for Rumi's activities and achievements. Its madrase provided both his father and him with a forum to lecture on Islam; in time Rumi was to become an extremely popular and influential speaker. Later he was to encounter his spiritual partner Shams al-Din of Tabriz in the streets of Konya and undergo his strange metamorphosis under Shams' influence into a great mystic and poet there. And it also was in Konya that Rumi, toward the end of his life, produced his masterpiece the *Mathnawi*, and then passed away.

57

Resting about five thousand feet above sea level, Konya quite likely was attractive to the family because it seemed to be invulnerable to the assaults of the Mongols. The city also boasted a long and fascinating history. Nine thousand years ago it was the site of an Anatolian community that worshipped a mother goddess much like the future cults of Artemis and Diana. It subsequently became an important city of the Roman Empire and later was visited by Jesus' disciple, St. Paul who preached there. Still later, Anatolia became the capital of the Seljuk Empire of Rum, from which the poet's name, Rumi, derives. All these varied and rich cultural and religious influences in time would find their way into Rumi's writing.

The Valad family also appears to have chosen to settle in Konya because Baha al-Din had received a position at Altunpa Madrase there; the exact nature of his post is unclear, but the scholar Franklin Lewis suggests he taught religious, rather than legal, subjects. The madrase may have been rather new because at this time the Seljuk dynasty was funding new seminaries in Anatolia. The Seljuks also had built a new palace and citadel and completed the construction of a great mosque in the city. It appears that other refugees from Khorosan also were attracted to this region by its opportunities and hospitable environment. Finally, Baha al-Din, in his last years, obtained the sort of stable, respectable post that had eluded him at many earlier points of his life.

Rumi appears to have served as his father's assistant at the madrase, perhaps helping him to teach his classes and sitting beside him, a gesture which may have indicated Baha al-Din regarded his son as his successor. There isn't much evidence that Rumi had delved seriously into mysticism before this time, and there is no suggestion that he had begun to write poetry. Until his early twenties, and during these years at the madrase, he seems to have concentrated, under his father's supervision, on

Genghis Khan and his sons Rashid al-Din
(d. 1318). Persian manuscript.
(Art Resource, NY)

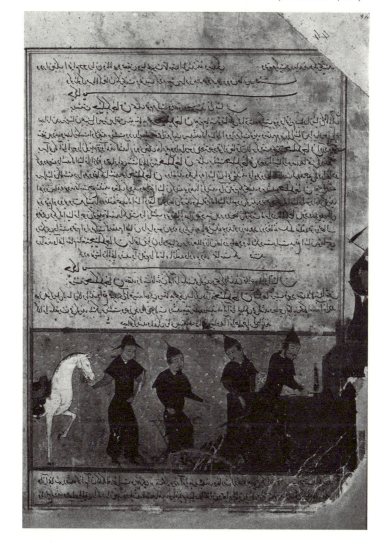

Islamic law and other hard sciences. In time, Rumi, in marked contrast to his father, would come to be known as a solid legal thinker.

In about 1231, perhaps two years after settling in Konya, Baha al-Din passed away. At the time he was probably about eighty-four years old and Rumi about twenty-four. For Rumi, the loss of the man who was both his mentor and his father—a man he also viewed as a great saint—must have been very sorrowful. Yet, soon Rumi was to acquire a new mentor, who advanced the future poet's education in ways that his father had not.

A year or so later following the death of Baha al-Din, a man who had been his disciple in Khorosan, Sayyed Borhan al-Din Mohaqqeq, turned up in Konya. The fifteenth-century hagiographer Dowlatshah alleges that Borhan al-Din had accompanied the family on part of its trek, traveling with them as far as Mecca, and on to Syria, but it is unclear whether he actually did so. Other historians indicate that Borhan al-Din had not seen the Valad family for about fifteen years, when he arrived in Konya, and that he had last seen Rumi when he was a child of ten or so.

It is possible that Borhan al-Din had been searching for his old teacher when he arrived in Konya, and had not realized that Baha al-Din had died. After reuniting with the Valad family, he took up the task of educating Rumi where Baha al-Din had left off. He was to serve as Rumi's mentor for about a decade, until Rumi was able to take over his father's station at the madrase.

Rumi later described Borhan al-Din as very capable in his reasoning and able to argue well, suggesting, perhaps, that this teacher taught Rumi the finer points of legal arguments. But Borhan al-Din also was adept with spiritual matters and experienced with fasting and other disciplines and mortifications used to achieve a transcendent state of being. Borhan al-Din believed that refraining from eating led to detachment from worldly matters. He once wrote: "The lamp of the light of faith is lit within the glass of the body of the believer. The body of the gnostic through self-abnegation becomes just like a glass through which the light of faith shines . . ."[2] The hagiographer Aflaki depicted Borhan al-Din as fanatical on the subject of fasting, and also suggested that he had poor hygiene. Under his strict tutelage, Rumi's experience and understanding of mysticism were to develop a great deal.

In Borhan al-Din's care, Rumi, for the first time, read his father's book the *Ma'aref* and began to learn in depth about the mystical aspect of Baha al-Din's spiritual life. It is a mystery why Baha al-Din himself did not instruct Rumi much in mystical teachings and practices, but he may have wanted to wait until his son was older. Like other Islamic mystics, Borhan al-Din emphasized self-conquest over one's carnal nature and overcoming one's "nafs," or worldly desires. "When you act contrary to the concupiscent soul, Almighty God is at peace with you: when you make peace with the self, you are at war with God," he once wrote.[3]

If Aflaki is to be believed, the teacher recommended a number of fairly extreme mystical practices to Rumi, and the student was only too glad to oblige. According to the hagiographer, Borhan al-Din once told Rumi to sit in a sealed room for a week and fast. Rising to the challenge, Rumi supposedly volunteered to sit in such a room with only a pitcher of water and some bread for a full forty days.

In Aflaki's account, Borhan al-Din entered the room after the forty days had passed; Rumi, lost in a mystical trance, did not respond to him. So the teacher decided to leave Rumi alone in the sealed room for another forty-day stretch, at the end of which, Borhan al-Din again entered the chamber and again was ignored by the blissful student. Another consecutive forty-day fast ensued, and at the end of this period, the teacher tore down the door and found Rumi smiling back at him. Although Aflaki's story is beyond far-fetched, Sultan Valad indicated that Rumi spent much of the five years following the death of Baha al-Din in fasting. It also is clear from other accounts that for much of his life Rumi attached great importance to fasting.

There is another, somewhat more credible story told by Aflaki in which Rumi, now quite advanced in years, catches sight of his own emaciated physique in a bath house and exclaims: "I have never felt embarrassed by anyone before except now that I see how much my body has become thin. . . . What could I say? My peace of mind rests on the fatigue I impose on my body. Should I get one moment of peace, my soul would not."[4]

BORHAN AL-DIN SEEMS to have thought that the madrase in Konya was not sufficiently distinguished for Rumi, given the young man's bright prospects. So he arranged to send Rumi to Syria to acquire a first-class Islamic education at some of the older and more venerable seminaries there. Rumi's excellent education, in time, would give him a credibility his father sometimes lacked, enabling him to earn widespread respect and a large following when he later returned for good to teach at the madrase in Konya.

Borhan al-Din also was willing to help make alternate arrangements so that the students of Baha al-Din at the madrase could continue their studies while Rumi was away. He may have done some of the teaching himself. The record is not absolutely clear on where in Syria Rumi studied; there are indications he studied in Aleppo, but there is other evidence he went to Damascus. It also is possible he spent time in institutions in both cities. At such schools Rumi would have lived solitarily in a small cell. The historian Franklin Lewis notes that Rumi would have had to leave his small sons, then about six and eight years old, behind in the care of other relatives. He also suggests that the spiritual leadership of the family during this period may have been left to Rumi's mother-in-law, who had been one of the leading disciples of Baha al-Din. There also are signs that Borhan al-Din helped look after Rumi's family.

According to Aflaki, Rumi went to study at the Halaviye mosque in Aleppo under the famous Hanafi scholar Kamal al-Din Ibn al-Adim, sometime between 1232 and 1233. Ibn al-Adim reportedly was a jurisconsultant of considerable influence. If this piece of information is accurate, he would have been of great help to Rumi in establishing his legal studies and credentials. Aflaki also relates a very dubious but highly entertaining tale about Ibn al-Adim being teleported out of town after witnessing Rumi's miraculous powers. After this remarkable exploit, Ibn al-Adim and the entire population of Aleppo became disciples of Rumi. Aflaki claims that Rumi's popularity in Aleppo was so intense and distracting that it became necessary for him to depart for Damascus to continue his studies in peace.

Rumi, now en route to Damascus, as Aflaki continues the account, next encountered a band of forty Christian "Desert Father" monks in a cave. These wondrous monks all had the abilities of reading minds, predicting the future, and levitation. They instructed a child to levitate for Rumi's benefit. Not to be outdone, Rumi, apparently through his superior mental powers, suspended the child in midair. Rumi did not release the child until he proclaimed himself a Muslim. If Rumi indeed spent time in Damascus, there is confusion about the length of his stay. He may have stayed there either for four years or for seven years. It also is possible he made more than one trip to Damascus during the decade after the death of his father.

According to the *Maqalat* of Shams al-Din of Tabriz, Rumi and Shams may have met ever so briefly in Damascus during

Sufism Attracting Many Women Followers and Saints

Since its inception, Sufism has had its share of women saints and practitioners. By legend, the Spanish mystic Mohyi al-Din Ibn Arabi, a contemporary of Rumi, once was asked how many "substitutes" (saints) there were. He supposedly answered that there were forty "souls." Asked why he did not say forty men, he answered that some were women. However, the Islamic cultural tradition of concealment for women has allowed some of these female saints to pass into anonymity.

Within Rumi's immediate family there were several women who were noted Sufi adepts, including the mother of his first wife. Rumi's mother-in-law was widely considered his spiritual equal and it was likely for this reason that he was married to her daughter, Gowhar Khatun. Rumi later arranged for his favorite female disciple Fateme Khatun, the daughter of his beloved friend Salah al-Din, to marry his favorite son Sultan Valad. Two girls were born of this marriage, Motahhare Khatun and Sharaf Khatun, and they apparently were especially precious to Rumi. In time, these girls grew up to be saintly women known in Konya for producing miracles and providing spiritual instruction to other women, according to Aflaki.

One of the earliest Sufi women saints whose life was recorded by historians was Rabi'a al-Adawiyya of Basra, who lived in the ninth century. She later was praised by the hagiographer Abd al-Rahman Jami for the brilliance and sincere humility she displayed in conversation. She also was praised by the writer Attar.

Once Rabi'a al-Adawiyya was approached by a man seeking the way, who asked her to provide him with security. Immediately, she began to weep, according to Jami. The man seemed quite stunned and asked her why she was crying. She reprimanded him, observing that security in this world entails the abandonment of God. Through his inquiry the man had defiled himself, according to the saint. On another occasion, the same man told her that they had been "saddened by God." The saint asked him not to lie, noting that if he had been so saddened he would not be able to enjoy the world as he then was.

Jami also tells the story of a thirteenth-century Andalusian woman saint named Fidda who became famous for performing miracles. Once a visitor to her village learned she had a goat that dispensed both milk and honey. He met Fidda and gave her a jar and asked her to fill it with milk and honey from her goat. She complied and he drank milk that was filled with honey. The guest then asked Fidda how such a miracle could have been performed. She explained that once her husband had been preparing to slaughter the goat as an offering at the end of Ramadan. However, she convinced her husband not to kill the goat because they were a poor couple and poverty is an excuse for not making offerings. The very same day a guest arrived, and the husband concluded that he must slaughter the goat in order to feed the guest. However, in the moment that the husband was sacrificing the goat, another goat appeared and entered Fidda's house. The new goat was to provide the couple with milk and honey.

Fidda concluded that when disciples, such as herself and her husband, have hearts that are pure and good, their ability to perceive is elevated, and even milk can taste like honey.

In general, Sufi women saints were not from the highest classes. However, in the seventeenth century in India, a princess converted to Sufism. She was named Jahanara and was a daughter of the Mughal emperor Shahjahan, the builder of the Taj Mahal. Jahanara considered herself the disciple of Mu'in al-Din Christi, a famous Indian Sufi who died four centuries before her birth. The Christi Order attracted many women followers and saints, although the princess was the most famous. She later produced a written account of her mystic connection with her late master that is one of the few Sufi surviving writings by a woman.

Unlike the surviving Mevlevi groups in Turkey and Iran, women comprise a large portion of the memberships of newer Mevlevi organizations in Europe, the United States and South America. Ironically, the Turkish government's severe restrictions on Sufism and *sama*, have led to some unexpected opportunities for Western women. The government tolerates performances by whirling dervishes chiefly as a tourist attraction and tends to be more lenient to visitors to Turkey interested in the sacred dance than to Turkish citizens who wish to practice Sufism. In 1994 a group of twenty-two members of the Mevlevi Order of America, including fourteen women, were allowed to perform the dance in the sacred *sama* hall of the Mevlevi complex in Konya. Even without the presence of women this would have been a rare event, given that Turkish authorities remain anxious about actual religious ceremonies taking place in the complex's traditional *sama* hall, although supervised performances are permitted elsewhere in Konya.

those years. Shams refers to a passing and insignificant meeting between the two men during those years. If this encounter indeed took place, Rumi may not have remembered it later when the two men had their legendary, and supposedly "first" encounter in Konya. There also is speculation that during a visit to Damascus, Rumi met great thinkers of the period, including Ibn Arabi, the famous Spanish Sufi mystic whose writings had pantheistic overtones and who argued that the universe is an extension of God's being.

Rumi appears to have returned to Konya for good after perhaps eight years of intermittent study abroad under Borhan al-Din's instruction. According to Aflaki, Rumi, upon his return was invited to live at the estate of a local prince, Saheb-e Esfahani. However, Borhan al-Din supposedly advised him not to accept this offer—noting that the modest Baha al-Din had resided at the madrase in Konya.

The hagiographers tell us that, after completing his supervision of Rumi's education, Borhan al-Din wished to leave Konya for Kayseri, but Rumi begged not to be parted from his beloved teacher. Borhan al-Din went anyway, but had an accident that forced him to return to Konya. He finally managed to move to Kayseri for good by asserting that, given Rumi's greatness, there was no need for both men in Konya. Franklin Lewis suggests that Borhan probably wanted Rumi to assume his father, Baha al-Din's position, but Rumi, in deference to Borhan, would not have been comfortable doing so while his teacher was in residence.

There are some quite humorous accounts of Borhan al-Din—the once uncompromising ascetic—relaxing considerably and neglecting his fasting and prayers in later years. Some say he grew quite fat. According to the chronology presented by Sultan Valad, Borhan died either in 1240 or 1241, after which Rumi began another long period of fasting. However, others believe

Borhan al-Din around 1240, left Konya for Kayseri, and that he died there in 1245.

Rumi was about thirty-four years old when he returned to Konya to live permanently and to take up his father's post at the madrase. His first wife, Gowhar Khatun, was to die a bit later, around 1242 or 1243, after having spent a good part of the final years of her marriage separated from Rumi as he pursued his studies in Syria. The nature and quality of Rumi's relationship to his first wife remain a mystery. Few medieval writers, in the Islamic or Christian worlds, bothered to include the details of their domestic lives in their writings, and the poet was no exception. A bit more can be gleaned about Rumi's second wife, the much younger Kerra Khatun, although much of this information comes from sources other than Rumi himself.

References to marriage, and women in general, in Rumi's writings are veiled, complex and contradictory. Vast differences in culture and period make it very difficult for modern readers to form definite conclusions on this subject. Annemarie Schimmel points out instances in which Rumi, apparently following the tradition of the Prophet Mohammad, advises men to seek the advice of women, and then do the opposite of what was recommended. This advice reflected the widespread medieval conviction that women were less intelligent than men.

There also are passages—quite obnoxious by contemporary Western standards—in which Rumi suggests that women, by virtue of their supposed combination of wretched, innate inferiority and witch-like temperament, inadvertently lead men closer to their God, by creating dreadful situations that men must nobly rise above. In the *Discourses* he writes:

What is that way? To wed women, so that he might endure the tyranny of women and hear their absurdities, for them to ride roughshod over him, and so for him to refine his own character. "Surely thou art upon a mighty morality." By enduring and putting up with the tyranny of women it is as though you rub off your own impurity on them. Your character becomes good through forbearance; their character becomes bad through domineering and aggression.[5]

This disparaging view of women was so commonplace in medieval society that it is hard to even decide whether Rumi was putting forth his own thoughts, or merely mirroring conventional ideas. It also is impossible to know whether the poet was referring to his own marriage or not; the entire passage may be purely a Koranic commentary. Part of the pleasure, but also the frustration, of reading Rumi is the mercurial and fluid nature of his narration. His poetic voice darts from place to place, and idea to idea in such a manner that it is sometimes hard to know if he is embracing a concept or merely describing it.

Underscoring the difficulty of learning Rumi's true views of women, Schimmel notes other passages in which Rumi celebrated women as full of mildness and love, and criticized men as consumed with anger and lust. For instance, in the *Mathnawi*, Rumi writes:

Love and tenderness are human qualities.
Woman is a ray of God: she is not the earthy beloved.
She is creative: you might say she is not created.[6]

Whatever his personal views, Rumi, like his father, accepted women as disciples and took their spirituality quite seriously. Household status aside, women appear to have received roughly equal consideration as students of religion. Rumi wrote quite a few letters to his female disciples, and these are unfailingly warm and respectful.

For a modern Western reader, it is ironic that it is easier to learn something about Gowhar Khatun's mother as an individual than it is about the first wife of Rumi or his own mother. Yet there was a good reason Rumi's first mother-in-law was mentioned more often than his closer female relatives: Gowhar Khatun's mother was a distinguished disciple of Baha al-Din and it was in the realm of spiritual inquiry that medieval Islamic women distinguished themselves and achieved respect. Of course, it is possible that Rumi in fact saw women in general, and wives in particular, as menacing moral inferiors. For all we know he may have regarded Gowhar Katun as a torment; but then again, he may have considered her an angel.

Like other medieval Sufi writers, Rumi, in his poetry, mentioned actual living women very little and most often in connection with their spirituality, such as the story of the beautiful girl saved from the rape of Samarqand. The other women depicted by Rumi are allegorical figures, creatures of myth about whom he spun tales to convey larger truths about his God, his morality and his times. These characters, ranging from the Virgin Mary to the most scheming and lustful of adulterous wives, are thoroughly absorbing to read about. But these fictional creations tell us little about the women in Rumi's own life, a state of affairs thoroughly in keeping with medieval Islamic society and with the poet's own discrete and subtle nature.

6

Friend to Kings and Ruffians

The king was in the belvedere, expecting to see that
which had been shown mysteriously.
He saw a person excellent and worshipful,
a sun amidst a shadow.[1]

—*Jalalu'ddin Rumi*

THE MONGOL INVASION FINALLY caught up with Rumi and his
family in 1242 when the local Seljuk rulers of Konya realized
that they could not put up a successful defense against the
marauders' fierce army. The Mongols, in the early 1240s, overtook other Anatolian cities, including Erzerum and Sivas, leaving their usual trail of butchery in the region. Kayseri was pil-
laged in an especially viscous attack in which all male citizens
were killed. To avoid such a fate, the leaders of Konya decided
to pay tribute to the attackers.

The Seljuk leader of Konya, the prince Ghiyasoddin
Keykhosrow, was not in a position to fight. He had ruled the area
since 1237, apparently in a thoroughly ineffectual manner. The
prince had been badly undermined by a group of scheming
Kharezmians, who had settled in Anatolia after fleeing Khorosan
at the time the Mongols invaded their home. The Kharezmians
formed alliances with groups of odd self-styled mystics who were
endeavoring to ingratiate themselves with the area's poor and stir
up a revolt against the Seljuks. Already weakened by the large
number and surprising variety of local insurgents, the prince mere-

ly gave in to the Mongols. The surrender spared the citizens of Konya from the carnage that the Mongols typically left in their wake, yet they were to find themselves under oppressive new political leadership. The Seljuks remained political leaders in name only, serving as a kind of puppet regime for the Mongols.

Ghiyasoddin Keykhosrow died in 1245, leaving three sons. These sons eventually formed a triumvirate and were recognized by the Mongols in 1251. Yet they, too, were weak and spent much of their time feuding among themselves. In time one of the sons was murdered, and the other two became mere figureheads for the Mongols. Only one son was to survive long under the Mongols, and he ultimately was put to death by his vassal in 1267. After the Seljuks caved in, Mongol soldiers occupied the streets of Konya. They dismantled former Seljuk forts, but largely left the citizens alone.

In Aflaki's version of events, the Mongols' reticence to harm the people of Konya stemmed from a special mystical encounter with Rumi. Supposedly, the Mongols had intended to attack Konya brutally on a morning when Rumi had climbed a hill to perform a dawn prayer. The tent of the Mongol attackers had been set up directly underneath the hill and the soldiers had glimpsed Rumi immersed in a prayer so serene and deep that he was oblivious to the surrounding frenzy. We are told that the Mongols advanced toward Rumi and prepared to attack him with arrows. But somehow they were strangely unable to draw their bows. They then tried to ride their horses up the hill, but the horses all mysteriously refused to move.

Angered by the inexplicable circumstances, the army's general mounted his horse and resolved to attack Rumi himself. However, three times in a row he was unable to get his horse to mount the hill. Forced to admit that he had seen a true miracle, the general declared an end to the siege and forgave the city.

Whatever the truth of this chronicle, Rumi went on to maintain good relations with both the remaining Seljuks who served under Mongol supervision, and with the Mongols themselves. The presence in Konya of the invaders whom Rumi's family had for decades tried to evade could hardly have pleased him. Yet he avoided provocative confrontation, taking the view that religious scholars are above the fray of secular politics and should provide instruction to political leaders.

In his *Discourses*, Rumi often reflected on the nature of power, and the relationships between men of spiritual learning, and their leaders. In one passage he wrote: "The prophet, on whom be peace, said: 'The worst of scholars is he who visits princes, and the best of princes is he who visits scholars. Happy is the prince who stands at the poor man's door, and wretched is the poor man who stands at the door of the prince.' "[2] In this excerpt, Rumi concludes that in every encounter between a prince and a spiritual scholar, it is the scholar who, due to his superior spiritual wealth, has something to give, while the prince, occupying the inferior position, can only receive. This imbalance makes the scholar independent of the prince, in Rumi's thinking. He continues:

> He [the scholar] is like a light-giving sun whose whole function is giving and dispensing universally, converting stones into rubies and cornelians, changing mountains of earth into mines of copper and gold and silver and iron, making the earth fresh and verdant, bestowing upon the trees fruits of diverse kinds.

Rumi addressed specific passages of the *Discourses* to Seljuk and Mongol rulers. In one fascinating instance, he recalls a warning he apparently made to the Mongol Amir Parvana not to make alliances with the Tartars that would harm the Syrians and the Egyptians, because such an alliance inevitably also would undermine Islam. Rumi describes the Amir as heeding his words and thanking him for his counsel.

This scene, in which the wise Rumi offers the Amir sound advice and is thanked for doing so, provides a sharp contrast to his father Baha al-Din's ringing, unheeded denunciations of the Khwarazmshah. With his fine education, beautiful manner of speaking and exceptional personal charm, Rumi evidently was perceived by both the Seljuks and the Mongols as an important advisor.

THE YEARS RIGHT before Rumi's fateful encounter with Shams al-Din of Tabriz also were the years that Rumi occupied himself most intensely with his teaching at the madrase. From the time Rumi, around the age of thirty-four, took up his father's post, until his fateful encounter with Shams al-Din of Tabriz in his thirty-seventh year, Rumi dressed the part of a conventional professor in the traditional turban and gown. He was enormously popular with students of all backgrounds. In his lectures, Rumi brought the teachings of Islam to life. Worried about a tendency to reduce the religion to mere dogma, Rumi tried to convey to his listeners with his own being an ideal example of what it means to live the tenets of the Koran.

Before taking up music and poetry, which he would soon do after meeting Shams, Rumi was a religious reformer, albeit a very pious one who relied on the Koran, in all matters, and tried to teach others to follow its spirit, not just read its words. His chief aim was to help his disciples follow the example of the Prophet and not succumb to extraneous and corrupting influences. By many accounts, he would have achieved some degree of historical fame as a restorer of Islam, even if he had never taken up poetry.

Afzal Iqbal describes Rumi at age thirty-four as an "acknowledged leader of men." He tells us that Rumi "had won for himself recognition as an authority on religion—a subject on which he spoke with passionate eloquence and penetrating sincerity."[3] Iqbal also notes that Rumi was sought out by powerful persons, but that the poet's circle also was an open assembly that anyone could join; Rumi felt at home "with ruffians, the tailors and the shopkeepers."

Rumi's mid-thirties were also the years of his remarriage. Although the Koran permits up to four marriages, there is no indication that Rumi ever considered marriage to more than one woman at a time. His second wife, Kerra Khatun, like Rumi, had been widowed. She brought to the marriage two children, and during the 1240s she and Rumi produced a son, Mozaffar al-Din Amir Alem Chelebi, and a daughter, Maleke Khatun. Unlike Rumi's sons by his first wife, Mozaffar al-Din Amir Alem Chelebi received some religious training, but pursued a career in the government. In time, he abandoned his career and became a dervish. Rumi's daughter married a businessman.

The hagiographers describe Kerra Khatun as a peerless beauty and a woman with a very charming manner; again it is hard to know whether they were reporting clear facts, or burnishing Rumi's legend. Her ethnic and religious backgrounds also are difficult to establish. Some historians believe she may have been a Christian of Armenian, Greek or Turkish background; but others doubt this and believe she, too, was a Muslim.

By one account Kerra Khatun believed in genies, a common enough belief in medieval Anatolia. Aflaki tells us that she once complained of genies living in the family's house, and told Rumi that they were upset by her husband's habit of burning candles late into the night in order to read the *Ma'aref* of Baha al-Din. Apparently she was worried that the mischievous genies would launch some sort of retaliation against the members of the household. According to Aflaki, Rumi smoothed out the situation several days later by announcing to his wife that the genies had come to like him and even had become his disciples; this

Exterior. Tomb of Rumi, founder of the Mevlevi Order
of mystics, the Whirling Dervishes.
(Vanni/Art Resource, NY)

Aaref Chelebi leaving his ancestor's mausoleum at the head of a crowd, in ecstacy of music and dance. From Tardjome-i-Thevakib by the Mevlevi Dervish Aflaki. Bagdad, c. 1594. (Pierpont Morgan Library/Art Resource, NY)

being the case, they would not harm the family, he said.[4]

To a modern reader this anecdote appears to be a droll yarn in which Rumi shows himself to be a clever psychologist, calming his wife's anxieties without commenting on the absurdity of her beliefs. Yet the belief in genies—invisible vapors and other substances that permeate a place with good or bad fortune—was very influential in Anatolia. There is perhaps a small chance that Rumi, ever open-minded, took his wife's concerns seriously.

However, another Aflaki anecdote about Rumi and Kerra Khatun defies belief. According to Aflaki, Kerra Khatun was upset with Rumi because their sex life was dwindling as he pursued his fasting and other spiritual practices. Aflaki quotes her as confiding to another woman: "For this reason, he does no even look in my direction and does not attach importance to physical beauty. I wonder if any traces of human quality and marital lust are left in him, or if his appetites have left him entirely and he has abandoned them."[5] Aflaki proclaims Rumi divined his wife's thoughts and that very evening approached her with an insatiable sexual appetite, making love to her seventy times. In desperation, Kerra Khatun tried to run away to the roof of the house to avoid her inexhaustible husband. But Rumi pursued her, announcing he was not done yet. From this vignette, Aflaki draws the lessons that the men of God are capable of doing anything they choose to do, and also are attentive to the needs of others.

Here again, we have a tale so wild and improbable that it cannot be used to draw any sort of serious conclusion about the poet or, in this case, his second wife. Yet it is hard not to wonder if Kerra Khatun much of the time, found herself neglected by her distracted, ascetic husband. It does appear though that Rumi looked after his stepchildren, the children of Kerra Khatun's first marriage, and that they were buried alongside his blood relatives in his tomb.

DURING HIS MID-THIRTIES, Rumi was very accessible to his many students, who came from all levels of society. A number of anecdotes from Aflaki reveal Rumi's tolerant and broad-minded attitudes and his courteous ways, and help explain his popularity. In one story, Rumi is criticized by a member of the ulema for his supposedly strange habit of accepting disciples from humble and even questionable social backgrounds. "Were my disciples good men of eminence, I would have been their disciple!" he replied. "Since they are bad men, they accept my leadership so that I may change them."[6]

Other anecdotes from Aflaki reveal Rumi's rare attunement to animals and plants, an affinity which over the centuries has inspired frequent comparisons with his near contemporary, the Christian mystic St. Francis of Assissi, who died when the poet was about twenty years old. In one such story Rumi asks a student to prepare a plate of sweets. The disciple then follows Rumi secretly to a cave and watches him place the plate near a bitch who recently gave birth to several puppies. When Rumi turns and finds his pupil watching him, he explains that the mother had given birth to puppies a week beforehand, but had not been able to leave them to look for food. According to Rumi, God had transmitted the bitch's complaints to him, so that he might help her.

In total, Rumi appears to have spent his mid-thirties leading a model and distinguished life: advising the Mongols without necessarily respecting them, tending to his family and his students, and maintaining a wide array of friendships with ordinary and extraordinary people, while also caring for animals. This life of order, distinction and conventionality was to come to an unexpected halt with the sudden arrival in Konya of the brilliant, unsettling and strange dervish, Shams al-Din of Tabriz.

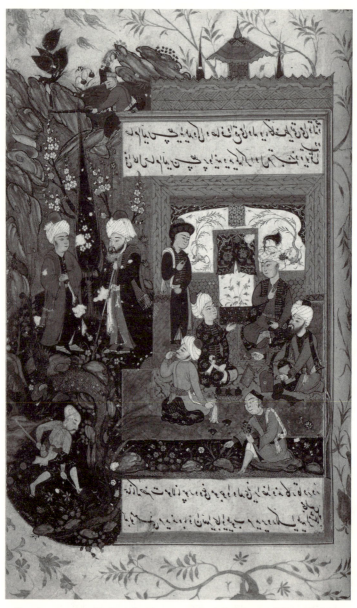

Rumi expressing his love for the young disciple Hosam al-Din Chelebi.
(Pierpont Morgan Library/Art Resource, NY)

7

A Love So Divine

Do not seek trouble and turmoil and bloodshed:
say no more concerning the Sun of Tabriz!
This [mystery] hath no end: tell of the beginning.
Go, relate the conclusion of this tale.[1]

—Jalalu'ddin Rumi

RUMI WAS TO SPEND MUCH OF his life trying to convey the "secret of the Friend," and "the [mystery] that hath no end," writing verse after verse in which he celebrated his passionate, mysterious relationship with Shams al-Din of Tabriz. The unorthodox friendship is widely credited with effecting the intense inner change that turned a conventional professor into an eccentric mystic who lapsed into long spells of speaking exquisite spontaneous poetry. There was nothing ordinary about Rumi's expansive, heartfelt, multi-tiered poetic visions and there was nothing ordinary about his dynamic, obsessive relationship to Shams. In the end, this unique "lover's secret" would be told "forth openly" and would disturb and change the lives of all in Rumi's circle.

In fact, the relationship was so extraordinary that some readers believe it never took place and that Shams didn't really exist. These skeptics think it possible that Shams was simply a literary creation of Rumi's—a theory much like the legend that Socrates was an invention by Plato. However, the historian Franklin Lewis notes that the existence of Shams' writing makes it hard to argue that he never existed. Other historians variously believe

Shams' existence could be proven by tombs in Iran, Turkey and Pakistan, all of which claim to contain his remains, although there is no consensus of opinion on these stakes.

In terms of literary models, the relationship calls to mind the 1950's Beat writer Jack Kerouac, who claimed he was not able to write until he encountered the charismatic vagabond Neal Cassady. Yet, the relationship of Rumi and Shams, although famous throughout the world for the poetry it inspired Rumi to write, was not primarily literary. And the difficult, asocial, profound Shams could hardly be described as a mere muse. The core of the relationship was the intense spiritual comfort the men found in each other. Rumi and Shams were mystical lovers and equals. Theirs was an intense spiritual love, celebrated by Rumi with some of the most extravagant love imagery ever produced. This poetry is in keeping with the conventions of Persian literature, which frequently celebrates an idealized Beloved in the form of a gorgeous youth, a custom adapted from Hellenic civilization. Yet Rumi's paeans to Shams also wreak havoc with these conventions, given that the sixty-year-old dervish was far from youthful or gorgeous at the time he met Rumi, and also was staunchly opposed to sexual relations with young men.

The famous relationship also completely altered Rumi's relationship to his society. Perhaps the highest-ranking member of the ulema in Konya and the very picture of professorial respectability, Rumi, on meeting Shams, abruptly lost interest in anyone or anything else, withdrawing into a kind of stunned, childlike state in which he fixated on the Friend.

Just who was this Sun of Tabriz, the Adored One who inspired Rumi to probe the mystery that hath no end? According to Reynold A. Nicholson, the great translator of the *Mathnawi*, there suddenly appeared in Konya on November 29, 1244, as if from nowhere, a "weird figure, wrapped in coarse black felt."

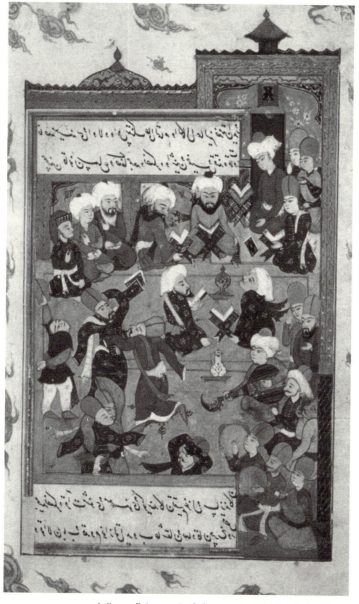

A "sama" (a mystical dance ceremony) of whirling
dervishes, during the leadership of Rumi's successor
Hosam al-Din Chelebi. 1590s, probably Baghdad.
(Pierpont Morgan Library/Art Resource, NY)

The dervish, then about sixty years old, apparently was as unattractive as Rumi was attractive, and as unpopular as Rumi was popular. Shams also seems to have worn an intense expression that many found frightening.

A wanderer from Tabriz in northern Iran with little interest in society, his manners probably were rough and abrasive. Nicholson characterized him as "comparatively illiterate." However, a few subsequent scholars have probed his writings, fairly recently published in Persian with scattered portions now available in English. These scholars have considered Shams' work well written and deep. But, none of this was to matter to Rumi, who was magnetized by Shams' profound spiritual state.

Shams was quite used to being thought odd. He, in turn, had little use for society. He once wrote: "I have no business with the common folk of the world; I have not come for their sake. Those people who are guides for the world unto God, I put my finger on their pulse."[2] The historian Golpinarli characterized Shams as a "qalandar," or wandering dervish unaffiliated with any particular order. This type of dervish was closely linked to a group called the *Malamatiyya*, whose members sought to purify themselves spiritually through aggressively seeking the condemnation of others. These dervishes would perform bizarre acts in public specifically to prompt criticism and disgust. If he indeed was affiliated with this group, Shams' unconventionality may have resulted from his principles as much as from his highly unusual nature.

An uncompromising, idealistic Muslim with no tolerance for hypocrisy in any form, Shams turned away from any mundane matter that might interrupt his all-consuming religious search. In Rumi he was to find a companion who also was thoroughly preoccupied with understanding the core of Islam and would endure no compromises in pursuing a correct religion.

APPARENTLY SHAMS HAD DISPLAYED strange spiritual leanings since childhood. In the compilation of his religious musings, the *Maqalat*, Shams portrays himself as having been a peculiar, unsociable youngster, who became fascinated with fasting even before reaching puberty. His otherworldliness separated him from others. His parents, whom he conceded were loving and kind, irritated him with their ordinariness and lack of spiritual awareness. He once described himself in relation to his parents as "a duck egg under a common hen age." He did not rate their simple goodness highly, valuing only the gnostic search.

In one section of his writings, Shams recollects his feelings of irritation when his father expressed parental concern that he may have fasted too much. He writes:

Father would say, "Alas for my son. He says he will eat nothing." I would say: "But, I'm not weak; I'm so strong that if you want I'll fly out of that window like a bird."

Every four days a little lethargy would overtake me for a while and I would leave. During this time no morsel of food would go down. "What's wrong with you?" "Nothing's wrong Am I crazy? Did I tear anyone's clothes? Did I fall on you? Did I rip your clothes?" "Aren't you going to eat?" "I'm not eating today." "Tomorrow, the day after, the next?"[3]

As a youth Shams, unlike Rumi, did not enjoy an elite education. Yet he was literate and well versed in Islam and Sufism. He, too, studied *feqh*, or Islamic law, although he followed the Shafe'i rite, while Rumi was of the Hanafi rite. Later in life, possessive disciples of Rumi, angry at the poet's extreme attachment to the dervish, suggested that Shams was dim-witted and that Rumi understood this and addressed poetry to him only to test his students' devotion. Yet Shams' lucid writings disprove this theory. Indeed Shams' writings—though clearly less extensive, and of less historical importance than Rumi's—are quite lively and informative. The *Maqalat* is available in its entirety only in Arabic and Persian, but Franklin Lewis has rendered a selection of intriguing passages of it into English in his biography, *Rumi, Past and Present, East and West.*

These swatches, many of which were written down by disciples during lectures Shams gave during his years in Konya, have a compelling tone. It's worth noting that Shams never authorized publication of these passages. However, in them one can glimpse the force and certainty of his powerful personality. His observations have the sharp clarity of a man who always knew exactly what he thought and never doubted that he was in the right. If Rumi was a poet of mercuriality, infinite digressions and microscopic subtleties, in Shams we encounter a linear thinker with a steel-trap mind that never veers far from its course.

Shams' observations also have a striking emotional honesty. His dismissive remarks about his simple, kindly father are tactless and unsettling. Indeed his singlemindedness and lack of appreciation border on the offensive; yet one never questions that these were his real sentiments. In other translated passages, Shams writes very movingly about the pathos and singularity of his own fate, and one can easily feel sympathy for this man who was to bear many insults and receive little compassion or understanding in his lifetime.

At any rate, in the *Maqalat* we encounter a blunt and profound mind, incapable of dissembling; and these qualities also have inspired the comparisons to Socrates, whose fierce and explicit truths also proved more than his society could tolerate.

According to Franklin Lewis, during Shams' childhood there were in Tabriz about seventy Sufi adepts who practiced in an experiential, nonintellectual manner. These Sufis were quite influential there and Shams may have absorbed some of this influence. Aflaki attributes part of Shams' mystical education to a "wise elder" named Pir-e Sallebaf, who would twirl the child around in a meditative dance called "sama." Later Shams would introduce Rumi to this sacred twirling—a controversial practice in the Islamic world.

In the *Maqalat* Shams mentions that during his student days he was impressed with a high-ranking judge, the Qazi of Damascus, Shams al-Din Kho'i. Apparently, he had hoped the judge would accept him for private tutoring, but he was rejected. So Shams became a teacher of young children. Here we find strange echoes of the fate of Baha al-Din, who also was not accepted by the elite lawyer-divines of his era and had to adjust his ambitions accordingly.

Some scholars believe that Shams as a young man in Tabriz took a wife, although, if so, her name is not known. These scholars also believe that this marriage produced children. If this family indeed existed, Shams must have abandoned it frequently later in life when he began his chronic wanderings.

SHAMS SPENT MUCH of his middle and older years traveling from city to city, searching for great mentors as he pursued his ascetic practices. According to the hagiographer Aflaki, Shams' wanderings took him to Baghdad, Damascus, Aleppo, Kayseri, Aqsara, Sivas, Erzerum and Erzincan. A severe critic, he heard many of the great sheikhs and lecturers of his era, but was for the most part bitterly disappointed in them.

During his period of wandering, Shams, while in Damascus around 1202–1204, may have met the famous Andalusian mystical theosophist Mohyi al-Din Ibn Arabi, author of the famous book *Meccan Revelations*. In his writings he mentions someone with a similar name. Shams was critical of the great thinker for appearing to place himself above the Prophet Mohammad. Shams also studied with someone he identified as "Sheikh Mohammad." He writes that he learned much from this teacher, but grew uncomfortable with him because he questioned whether the sheikh was a sincere Muslim. At one point Shams scolded this sheikh for implicitly claiming a higher station than that of the Prophet Mohammad. He comments: "I gained a great deal from him, but not as much as from you. [Rumi]. How different the pearl from the pebble! Except that the disciples have not recognized you at all and this is very strange!"[4]

Shams' critical turn of mind made him hesitant to identify himself as either a *faqih* (legal scholar), or a *faqir* (a Sufi practicing spiritual poverty), because he perceived all too well the shortcomings in both groups. Shams, who emerges in his writings as something of a malcontent, is particularly critical of the dervishes, many of whom he finds hollow. In the *Maqalat* he writes:

At first I wouldn't mix with jurists, only with the dervishes. I'd say that the jurists are ignorant of dervish-hood. Now that I have realized what dervish-hood is and what they are, I find myself more eager for the company of jurists than dervishes because the jurists have struggled to attain something. These others boast that they are dervishes. But where are the true dervishes?[5]

Unimpressed with most teachers he met, Shams claimed that he was an "Ovysi Sufi," an initiate who had received his spiritual knowledge directly from God, and not from any living teacher. Sepahsalar describes Shams during his wanderings as a marginal figure, isolated from others by deep spiritual abilities that few could fathom, so little a part of society that he seemed to be almost invisible. He writes that Shams was "hidden from the people, not claiming a station for himself."

According to Sepahsalar, it occurred to no one that Shams might be a great saint during the years before he met Rumi; the hagiographer even questioned whether anyone would ever truly grasp Shams' profound spirituality. He exclaims, "Before the time of his holiness our lord [Rumi], no creature was appraised of his [Shams'] state and even now no one will ever comprehend the truths of his mysteries." Before coming to Konya, he traveled about in an anonymous manner, attracting little attention, dressing like and fitting in with merchants, although he was not one. Sepahsalar tells us that Shams lodged at the caravanseries of merchants and wherever he stayed, would secure his humble room with a large lock, despite the fact he owned little and slept on straw mats. He "constantly hid his miracles."

The relationship that was to revolutionize his life apparently caught Rumi by complete surprise. In contrast, Shams for decades had been wandering throughout the Islamic world in search of such a Friend and seems almost to have preordained the friendship.

In the *Maqalat*, Shams describes his long, poignant search for spiritual companionship. Withdrawn and highly sensitive, Shams appears to have been a misfit, a lonely possessor of knowledge of life's inner mysteries. He tells us that his search for spiritual company was motivated in large part by this overwhelming sense of apartness. He writes: "I can talk to myself. I can talk with anyone in whom I see myself . . . I wanted someone of my own type to make into my qeble [the direction one faces in prayer], and turn to, for I had grown tired of myself. Do

Sufi Customs Play Strong Role

While it is easy for a Westerner to develop a view of the Sufis as free spirits, they in fact lead well-ordered lives in which custom plays a strong role. To give a simple example: one does not become a Sufi simply by showing up. There are detailed activities for neophytes and ceremonies of initiation, including "the bestowal of a cloak." During medieval times many Sufi orders had special ceremonies in which the sheikh of the local lodge would bestow an item of clothing as a rite of initiation.

The presentation of a cloak to a Sufi initiate also corresponded with customs of caliphate courts, where fine fabrics often were presented to subjects as tributes. The Sufis liked to cite a number of auspicious references in the Koran to cloaks and coats and other items of clothing which perform miraculous functions. The Koran and the Judeo-Christian Bible both mention an anecdote involving the multi-colored coat of the Prophet Joseph. The famous coat carried Joseph's scent, which helped to restore the eyesight of his blind father, Jakob. There is another story in the Koran in which Gabriel presents a cloak to the Prophet, and Mohammad wears this cloak as he ascends to heaven.

Some Sufi orders bestowed different types of cloaks to signify different levels of spiritual aspiration. For instance, there were "cloaks of longing," or discipleship, for serious disciples, as well as "cloaks of blessing," for persons interested in Sufism who are not yet ready for discipleship. Some orders also gave "cloaks of succession" to disciples who had become sheiks.

The significance of giving such items of clothing appears to be largely ceremonial, but ceremonies were seen by many Sufi orders as an important means of linking inner experience to proper behavior. And, for all their mysticism, Sufis take a detailed interest in external behavior. Most orders set forth a number of rules which bound members of the community. Sultan Valad set forth strict standards for the Mevlevi community after the deaths of his father and Hosam al-Din. The rules compiled by Sultan Valad concerned fasting and eating, begging for alms, how disciples should behave with each other, the master-disciple relationship, and how to control one's "nafs," or selfish impulses.

Other dervish orders came up with much more elaborate manuals of conduct that addressed a variety of daily life dilemmas for the dervishes, such as what to do with shirts that have been torn in ecstasy during performances of *sama*. Many of these manuals of conduct were so extensive that they weighed several pounds.

Over the centuries, there have been quite a few precise Sufi codes of conduct for enjoying *sama* and instrumental music. The topic of music has generated much controversy for Sufism, and Islam in general, largely because instrumental music was not a common or sophisticated art form in Arabia during the lifetime of Mohammad. Because there were no indications that Mohammad ever enjoyed musical performances, his spiritual descendants who liked music felt compelled to codify, and justify in extremely precise religious terms, how it could be enjoyed.

A thirteenth-century Sufi Persian mystic named Ruzbihan Baqli wrote an essay called "The Practices of Listening to Music," in which he concluded that the experience of hearing music varies for common people, the elite, and for "the elite of the elite. According to Baqli, common people listen with their physical nature, which corresponds to begging, while the elite listen with the heart, which represents seeking. However, in his view "the elite of the elite," listen with the soul, which signifies loving.

Later Pakistani Sufis produced a book called *The Melodies of Listening to Music*, which was published in English in 1972 and contains a code of ten precise rules for Sufi music lovers. According to these standards, singers and listeners must recite verses from the Koran before and after performances. They also must "sit properly," which means they should not stretch their feet, lean on something, or be cross-legged. The singer also should wear perfume, and should keep his eyes on the face of the master, to avoid losing his place, and must not indulge in unseemly displays of fake ecstasy.

Most importantly, according to this code, a singer or listener must "not let the divine attractions become disturbing or exciting." On the other hand, in the event that a listener is not moved by the singing, he should swiftly leave the assembly to avoid disturbing the music lovers.

you understand what I mean by having grown tired of myself? Then, having turned into a qeble, he would understand and comprehend what I am saying."⁶

In another passage, Shams writes about his intense pleasure in encountering Rumi, emphasizing that he traveled much of his life to find such a person. Quite extravagantly, he declares that he would rather see Rumi than have his late father brought back to life. Yet, strikingly, the unsparingly honest Shams also reveals that Rumi in some ways fell short of his ideal and concludes he has not yet met his "sheikh," or spiritual leader. His admission contrasts sharply with the words of Rumi, who issued a nearly endless string of superlatives in praise of Shams, never criticizing the Beloved.

Ever since he left Tabriz, Shams explains in the *Maqalat*, he had sought a sheikh, or spiritual leader, who would "give him a cloak"—a Sufi gesture by which a master accepts a disciple. Upon meeting Rumi, he found a man capable of bestowing cloaks, but hesitant to do so. Rumi never asked to give cloaks to disciples or formalize the master-disciple relationship in other ways. Shams says, "If they come up to him and oblige him saying 'Give me a Kherqe [cloak], shave off my hair,' he does so under duress. He is quite different from someone who says, 'Come be my disciple.'"

Yet, if begged, he sometimes relented and went through these sorts of ceremonial motions, but only for the sake of the disciple, according to Shams. By contrast, Rumi believed that a true sheikh would accept a disciple before the disciple understood the actual nature of the relationship. Shams tells us that Rumi was the sole person he has encountered in his travels with this profound understanding of the mentor-disciple relationship. Says Shams:

It was on account of this quality that I returned from Aleppo to be in his company. Whereas, suppose they had told me, "Your father has risen from the grave in the desire to see you and is come to el Basher [which is thirty miles outside Aleppo] to see you. Come and see him before he dies again." I would have said: "Tell him die, what can I do?" And I wouldn't have left Aleppo. But I came here for that quality of Rumi.[7]

By all accounts, the fateful meeting on November 29, 1244, when Rumi and Shams embarked on the "path beyond master and discipleship," was an event of cataclysmic proportions. The meeting was to leave the two mystics in thrall with one another and many of the citizens of Konya enraged by their exclusion from the charmed circle.

After studying a description of the meeting by Rumi's son Sultan Valad, who knew Shams personally, the writer Afzal Iqbal concludes that Rumi, in spite of all his prestige and knowledge, also had been in some sort of depression or rut and in need of spiritual company. He writes: "Shorn of all dramatic elements, the simple fact must be stressed that Rumi, himself on a high spiritual pedestal, was restless and was in quest of a man worthy of his confidence and so also was Shams." He goes on to say that both men being of "great spiritual eminence . . . they naturally discovered each other on account of their highly developed sense of intuition. Each felt like a traveler who reaches his destination after years of labor and toil." Iqbal also concludes that: "For Rumi it [the meeting with Shams] brought the dawn of a new world, a living pushing force, an élan vital, a divine sympathy, a feeling which penetrates the very essence of things. . . . From this day started the real work of Rumi, the work which has made him immortal."[8]

As Sultan Valad tells it, Shams' spiritual depth, his godliness, was so overwhelming that Rumi ceased to need other companions. For Rumi, looking at Shams was in some quite literal way like gazing at the sun or into the face of God. After meeting Shams, Rumi became entranced with what Sultan Valad described as the dervish's "majesty of God [that] kept him [Shams] hidden, remote from the sphere of imagination and thought." In time Rumi was to take up the massive task of transmitting his own understanding of Shams' veiled illumination to the world through verse. In the words of Afzal Iqbal, "This unique experience of consciousness set off the potential energy stored up in the reservoir."

In Sultan Valad's view, the arrival of Shams was a gift from God to Rumi. Borrowing from the conventions of Persian literature, Sultan Valad describes his father as falling madly in love with the dervish whom he believed to be a saint so visionary that only someone like Rumi could perceive his depths; ordinary people would try to encounter someone like Shams, but when they did, would not be able to comprehend him. But Rumi had been "singled out by God," to view the true face of Shams, and receive his piercing truths.

> Madly he fell in love with him and lost himself. All conflict born of logic [high and low] was resolved. He asked him to his house saying, "Listen to the pleading of this dervish, O king; although my abode is not worthy of you, yet in all sincerity I am your devoted slave, and whatever I possess [at present] and whatever I may happen to possess [in the future] is and will remain yours [by the grace of God.]"[9]

In the *Maqalat* Shams describes his crucial meeting with Rumi in Arabic, although he more frequently wrote in Persian. He discusses how he began by questioning Rumi about the case of Bistami, the Sufi celebrated by Attar, although considered blasphemous by many because he declared himself to be God. Shams asked Rumi if Bistami indeed did not need to follow the Prophet, or say "Glory be to Thee," or "We worship thee." Shams exclaims, "And Rumi completely understood the full implications of the problem and where it came from and where it was leading to. It made him inebriated on account of his purity of spirit. I realized the sweetness of this question from his inebriation, though I had been previously unaware of its sweetness."[10]

For Shams, posing the issues of Bistami's actions, and whether a Muslim must follow the Prophet unswervingly, provided a sort of acid test that enabled him to gauge Rumi's spiritual orientation. Shams, in posing these questions, was trying to learn whether Rumi was dominated by vanity, egotism or pleasure-seeking, or whether he was resolved to humbly and correctly follow the Prophet Mohammad.

It is significant that Rumi and Shams both strongly rejected this extreme vein of Sufism, and began their relationship by clarifying their views on the key issue of Bistami's ideas; Bistami's famous declaration that he was God offended Shams greatly, and also was one of the facets of Sufism that made the teaching controversial. Shams was quite militant on this point; elsewhere in his writings he states that he does not believe that Sufis such as Bistami or Ibn Arabi, who also did not teach strict adherence to the Prophet's teachings, deserved to be considered true followers. Shams believed that feigned humility or declaring oneself superior to the Prophet were the most grievous errors.

HAGIOGRAPHERS HAVE PROVIDED several fantastical versions of the legendary initial encounter between the two men. Although these stories can't possibly all be true, most are quite entertaining; and, through their extravagant distortions, they inadvertently also confirm our sense that the encounter was of historical importance.

A Sufi named Muhyid-Din Abdul Qadir, a contemporary of Sultan Valad, alleged that the two men met when Shams entered Rumi's house while Rumi was lecturing. Supposedly Shams regarded a pile of books and asked the impertinent question: "What is this?" Rumi curtly answered: "You don't know." The books suddenly and mysteriously caught fire. Bewildered, Rumi said, "What is this?" Shams then issued the trump line: "You don't know," and quietly walked away. Rumi, according to this legend, went in search of Shams but could not find him. There is another quite similar tale in which Shams, through some magic trick or another, summons a flood within Rumi's house.

The fifteenth-century writer Dowlatshah writes that the two men became acquainted one day when Rumi and his students passed a caravansary of sugar merchants with whom Shams lived. Whereby Shams asked Rumi, "What is the purpose of wisdom and knowledge?" "To follow and reach the Prophet," replied Rumi. "That is commonplace," said Shams. Supposedly Rumi then asked Shams to provide his own definition of knowledge and Shams replied, "Knowledge is that which takes you to its source." Lastly, Shams quoted this bit from Sana'i: "Ignorance is far better than the knowledge which does not take you away from yourself." According to Dowlatshah, Rumi was so impressed with Shams' reply that he instantly became his disciple.

By Shams' own account he was an exceedingly possessive and domineering companion. Rumi's disciples and friends were quite correct in perceiving that their beloved teacher no longer belonged to them. Shams evidently felt it necessary to conduct a series of odd tests of Rumi's sincerity and spirituality, and one of his demands was for a severe kind of metaphysical exclusivity bordering on the bizarre.

In the *Maqalat* Shams tells about how during his pre-Konya travels he at one point had considered a sheikh named Owhad al-Din Kermani for the role of his special spiritual companion. However, he then rejected this prospect in large part because Owhad al-Din Kermani was, in Shams' view, overly attached to his students and would not have submitted to the dictates of an exclusive friendship. Shams writes:

> Owhad al-Din told me, "How about if you come and stay with me?" I said: "I'll bring a wine glass, one for me, one for you, and we'll circulate them round when everyone is gathered for sama [meditative dance]." He said: "I can't do it." I said: "Then you are no match for my company. You must give up your disciples and the whole world for a chalice."[11]

In this instance, there is no reason to think that Shams, a pious Muslim, actually drank wine, which is forbidden by the Koran. However, images of wine and inebriation are commonplace in the writings of Sufism in large part because many Sufis—and here one thinks of Attar—placed strong emphasis on the willingness to defy conventions in order to arrive at higher truths. Often the references to wine and drunkenness in Sufi poetry were purely allegorical. On the other hand, there were some Sufi lodges that tolerated alcohol. At any rate, in this instance, Shams seems to have been goading Owhad al-Din Kermani by mentioning wine and asking him to be willing to forgo the company of his students.

By legend, Shams' estimate of Owhad al-Din was to plummet further. Owhad al-Din, who apparently also shared the Hellenistic belief in the divine beauty of young boys, supposedly once told Shams, "I see the moon reflected in a vessel with water!" The remark was a metaphorical reference to the concept that the beauty of youths is a representation of the divine. The acerbic Shams snapped back, "If you have not got a boil on your neck, why don't you look at the sky?"

Some hagiographers tell a tale in which Shams, on first being brought to live in Rumi's home, asks for a glass of wine. An obedient Rumi immediately summons someone from the household to fetch a glass of wine. Shams then pushes the wine away and indicates that he never intended to drink it. The request was merely a test of Rumi's willingness to abandon accepted mores. By contrast to Owhad al-Din Kermani, Rumi's willingness to cast aside his students was thrilling to Shams.

The dervish took a strange pride in his extremely possessive attitude toward Rumi. Boastingly, he writes: "Whomever I love, I oppress. If he accepts it, I roll up like a ball in his lap. Faithfulness is something you practice with a five-year-old child. But the real thing is oppression."[12] At another point, Shams proclaims: "The person who enters my company is distinguished by the fact that he loses his appetite for company with others and finds it bitter. Not such that he loses his appetite and yet continues to keep company with them, but in such wise that he cannot keep their company."[13]

BY MOST ACCOUNTS RUMI, for his part, apparently submitted to Shams with great docility. He was aware of the impact on his students of the loss of his company, but seemed almost hypnotized by Shams and was unwilling to disobey him. Rumi, who in one verse described Shams as "the mouthpiece of God," seems to have considered Shams a divine presence to whom he should submit. According to Afzal Iqbal, shortly after Shams' arrival on the scene Rumi "did what he [Shams] bade him do." "He is reported to have said: 'When Shams al-Din first came, and I felt for him a mighty spark of love lit up in my heart, he took upon himself to command me in the most despotic and peremptory manner. "Keep silent," said he, "and speak to no one." I ceased all intercourse with my fellows.'"[14]

As most histories have it, Rumi invited Shams to come live with him in his house almost immediately after the two men met. There are descriptions by many historians and hagiographers of the two men spending countless hours by themselves at Rumi's home, basking in each of the others' company. The all-consuming nature of their friendship caused a distracted Rumi to neglect his household and students.

In some passages of his writing, Shams himself seems shocked by the deep change he brought about in Rumi, and the manner in which Rumi seemed to lose himself in Shams, forgetting all conventional considerations. In one account, Shams mentions his surprise that Rumi, who apparently in general was quite possessive of his young wife Kerra Khatun and usually shielded her from the attentions of all other males, allowed his wife to keep company with him. Shams describes Kerra Khatun sitting obediently near him like a child expecting a bit of food from her parent.

This powerful spiritual rapport cherished by Rumi and Shams, which angered and baffled many of the residents of Konya, was difficult even for the two men to define. At the time of their meeting in Konya, both men were mature. Shams at sixty was an old man by medieval standards and Rumi, about thirty-seven, was at the peak of his powers. Their maturity made it impossible for the two men to have a conventional Eastern master-disciple relationship because such arrangements generally begin when the disciple is still a youth.

In some passages, such as the one about his search for a "sheikh," Shams suggests that Rumi in many ways was the religious instructor he had long sought. Yet at other points he writes about

Rumi as if the poet were a pupil he was modeling into a spiritual ideal. There are glimpses of Shams in the role of the puppet master, contemplating quite deliberately how best to manipulate a puppet-like Rumi. There also are passages in both Rumi's and Shams' writings in which they refer to Shams as the light of the sun, while Rumi is depicted as the moon that reflects the intense sunlight. Shams once wrote that people cannot bear to look too long or hard at the intensity of the sun, but can focus longer on the gentler moon, a reference to Rumi's pleasing style of articulating Shams' harsh and bold truths. Because he believed that Rumi, with his eloquence, was the perfect medium to reflect his spiritual attainments to the world, Shams appears to have found it necessary to shape Rumi in various ways to prepare him for that role.

Rumi's evolution into a convention-defying mystic was no accident; a good deal of thought on the part of Shams preceded this transformation. Shams reveals a nearly missionary fervor in his determination to remove Rumi from the mundane, stifling confines of academia and turn him into a true "man of God." He complains that although Rumi is well versed in *feqh* (law), this knowledge has "no relationship to the path of God and the Prophets." Indeed, Rumi's legal background is a hindrance to his mystic development, in Shams' view. But the dervish adds that it would be unwise for him to confront Rumi directly about these points; instead, Rumi himself must come to be sick of legalistic thinking, and lose a bit of his ego, on his own accord. "One cannot say this to him. One must dissemble. He is just right for master and discipleship, though there are a hundred thousand such Mowlanas, whereas there is a path beyond master and discipleship."[15]

THE OUTRAGE THE PUPILS felt over Rumi's rhapsodic friendship with Shams was so intense that it, of itself, constituted a fascinating phenomenon; one of the oddities of Rumi's life and personality was the intensity of the jealousy and possessiveness he inspired, seemingly without effort. Not only did the disciples miss Rumi, there also is a sense that this was a love so special and profound that those excluded from it were made miserable by the mere thought of it. The students' anger was to reach feverish levels after Shams introduced Rumi to the controversial "sama"—or sacred twirling—accompanied by music.

Previously, Rumi, an ascetic like his father Baha al-Din and his teacher Borhan al-Din, had opposed music and dancing as being unacceptable for Muslims, citing the fact that there is no record of the Prophet Mohammad enjoying music and dance. However, Shams convinced Rumi that the prohibition against music and dance applied only to spiritually undeveloped persons because these enjoyments would spark lust and greed and other base desires in them. But—according to Shams—evolved Muslims could perform a meditative dance accompanied by either poetry or music because these pastimes would lead them to more intense levels of communion with God.

It is unclear what authority Shams cited for this view, which is quite inconsistent with a number of his other beliefs. Throughout his life, Shams was sharply critical of Bistami, Ibn Arabi, and others whom he suspected of not following the actions or spirit of the Prophet Mohammad. By his own account, he began his friendship with Rumi by clarifying what he believed to be the errors of Bistami in deviating from the Prophet's teachings. However, he apparently had practiced sama or its variants all his life, having learned to twirl as a child from the "wise elder" Sallebaf. So it is possible he never paused to ponder his own inconsistency.

In his efforts to transform Rumi, Shams pushed him to go beyond merely reading about mysticism, and to experiment with actual mystic practices, especially sama. Rumi later was to say Shams "set him on fire," and "burned his books," enabling him to transcend mere theoretical understanding. Some hagiographers tell a story in which Shams literally plunged all of Rumi's books into a fountain. In this tale, Rumi declines to retrieve his books because it would be tantamount to an acknowledgement that the world of knowledge meant more to him than the experience of ecstasy.

THE DANCE OF SAMA involves a very slow rotation, or twirling, in which every subtle body movement has mystic significance. For instance, the slow turning of the body represents the ability to perceive God from all angles and being enlightened from each part of God, while the stamping of the feet represents the crushing of the carnal nature.

In Shams' view, sama was very important for Rumi because it gave him a concrete experience of mysticism, forcing him to advance beyond the world of ideas. Shams did not believe that ideas, or words or science would, of themselves, lead one to truth. He considered the nature of a teacher more important than actual teachings and also believed there was no wisdom without love and emotional experiences. Sama was one of the most important means used by Shams to bring about Rumi's transformation. And, here again, we find the Sufi emphasis on willingness to transcend convention in search of more profound ideals.

Rumi quickly came to adore this form of music and dance. He and Shams would often twirl together during their sessions of mystic communion. Later, Rumi would scandalize much of Konya with the sight of the formerly upright professor flamboyantly enjoying the controversial practice in public for hours—at the same time that he was losing interest in book learning. There also were reports that he sometimes enjoyed sama with female relatives, a lapse which, if true, would compound his breach of etiquette and religious law in the view of many of his contemporaries. In the fourth book of the *Mathnawi* Rumi celebrates the pleasures of sama, calling it a tool for shattering "the foot of the intellect" through ecstasy. He writes that love is "the sea of non-being" in which "the foot of the intellect is shattered."

Many disciples were horrified by Rumi's wild enthusiasm for sama recalling that in the past he had opposed the practice and counseled others to avoid it because it was not an established part of Islam. Of course, the widely disliked Shams was held responsible for Rumi's uncouth new pleasure. Some disciples complained to the authorities about Rumi's and Shams' indulgence in sama, but no action was taken against them; they appear to have been saved by Rumi's favorable standing with the powerful.

As well, Shams was widely hated for allegedly controlling access to Rumi. According to the hagiographers, there were accusations that anyone who wished to speak to Rumi had to seek permission from Shams. There is even a questionable story that Shams based his decision of whether to allow a disciple to meet with Rumi on whether or not the person provided a lavish gift.

In addition, some of the hagiographers tell a story in which Shams, at a large public meeting, expressed his impatience with the ulema's dependence on book learning. In this tale Rumi and Shams attended a meeting at a new monastery. They sat patiently for hours, as various scholars recited the words of seers that they had memorized from reading books. At length an impatient Shams rose to his feet to ask the group: "How much longer are you going to waste your time repeating the words of this or that scholar? When will you say, 'My heart was inspired by God?' Why are you walking with the staff of another? Where are your words and your works?"[16]

SULTAN VALAD REPORTS THAT Rumi was cursed to his face by some of the jealous students. "All wondered when he [Shams] would quit town or come to a wrathful end," he wrote. But from Shams' own writing we get a quite different picture. He reveals that he was aware of the intense jealousy of the disciples and sought to minimize it. He also shows that he was aware of the disparity between his social standing and that of Rumi. Despite his highly possessive nature, Shams insists that he took care not to appear in public with Rumi often in order not to anger people. He writes:

> I go everywhere alone, by myself and sit at every shop. I cannot bring him—a man who travels in the circles of the Mufti of the city—with me everywhere or into every shop. I stop in at every bathhouse [alone]. You know I have never acted sheikh-like, unmindful of your station, and said: "I'm going here whether you like it or not and if you are mine, you'll come with me." No, I do not demand whatever is difficult for you.[17]

Despite his efforts, Shams was to have little success in calming the emotions of the jealous disciples. Afzal Iqbal has suggested that the friendship between Rumi and Shams upset many people because it threatened their notions of class hierarchy. The idea that the most learned citizen of Konya preferred the company of an eccentric and unattractive dervish over that of ranking members of the ulema was interpreted by many as a personal insult; it was incomprehensible to many people that anyone of Rumi's stature would blithely set aside the centuries-old prestige of the ulema for the company of a dervish.

Through Rumi's verse, we learn that he was aware that many of his followers—and there were thousands of them—detested

Shams and that his friend was considering leaving Konya. Rumi evidently was painfully aware of the pressures on Shams and worried often that the dervish would leave him. Rumi later was to write: "You are the light of my house. Do not go away and leave me alone."

However, Shams, for reasons not fully clear, suddenly left Konya probably sometime in the spring of summer of 1246. Sepahsalar tells us that the extreme envy of Rumi's students was the chief reason he left town; this explanation has become commonplace in large part because Rumi believed it. His departure in the spring came not a full year after his arrival on November 29, 1245. Yet Shams had been able to accomplish much during that brief period: he at last had found the peerless Friend he had sought his entire life, and he had transformed that Friend thoroughly, turning a great intellectual into a great mystic.

Dancing, whirling dervish.
(Foto Marburg/Art Resource, NY)

8

Life After Love: The Departure of Shams

If once in this world I win a moment with you,
both worlds I'd trample under a dance of triumph.
Oh, Shams of Tabriz, in this world I'm so drunk—now
only stories of drunkenness and revelry pass my lips.[1]

—*Jalalu'ddin Rumi*

RUMI WAS SHATTERED BY the sudden disappearance of Shams and embittered by the pervasive jealousy that preceded the dervish's departure. If the disciples had thought that by driving Shams away they would regain Rumi's attention, they would quickly realize that this was not the case. The rest of his life was to be spent in efforts to regain the sense of ecstasy, "the stories of drunkenness and revelry," he had enjoyed with Shams.

The most foolish of the schemers probably had not yet realized that in Rumi's eyes, Shams was not the ugly, uneducated dervish that they loathed, but rather the Beloved, "the Sun of Tabriz, the spiritual king." More to the point, Rumi would never revert to playing the role of the solid, attentive professor he had performed so well before Shams' arrival in Konya. The dervish had changed him forever, and Shams' disappearance intensified Rumi's awareness of his need for Shams, estranging him further from his plotting students.

Unstrung by his loss, Rumi went into a state of great agitation, behaving like a heartbroken lover and asking everyone he saw for news of his lost love. There are many poignant descriptions from the hagiographers of Rumi in a shell-shocked state. From Shams' own writing we learn that he fled to Syria and had resigned himself to permanent separation from Rumi. He tells us that, though still besotted with Rumi, he had intended to embark on a new phase of his life far from Konya: "When I was in Aleppo, I was busy with prayers for Mowlana [Rumi]. I prayed a hundred prayers and brought things to mind that would increase my affection to the exclusion of things that would cool the affections, but I had no intention to come."[2]

In this passage, we come across an intriguing possibility that Shams' religious principles—and not the jealous disciples—were the reason behind his sudden decision to abandon Konya. Franklin Lewis points out that Shams was also known as "Shams-e parande," or "Shams the flier." Aflaki interpreted the title as an indication that Shams often traversed the universe through telekinesis. However, the designation could also be interpreted as signifying that Shams was part of a Sufi group known as "gnostics" or "birds" which often took sudden trips and believed that the pain of separation from one's spiritual mentor or Friend could force one to new stages of development. This suggests that Shams may have left Konya so that both he and Rumi could progress on their mystical paths.

Nonetheless, another of Rumi's biographers, Mohhamad-Ali Movahhed, believes that Shams' departure to Syria was a kind of calculated ploy. Movahhed has suggested that the dervish actually was conducting yet another test of Rumi's loyalty. Under this theory, the renewed separation would force Rumi to make even stronger declarations of his preference for Shams over the disciples, a gesture which would reinforce Shams' position. If this indeed was the real motive for Shams' removal, the strategy certainly paid off; Rumi was to make it abundantly clear where his affections lay in a lifelong outpouring of verses, such as this one from the *Divan-e*:

When my heart noticed Love's sea, suddenly it escaped me and leapt in, crying, "Save me!"

Tabriz's glory, the face of the Wild One is The Sun whose track all cloudy hearts follow.[3]

But whatever the motivation behind Shams' departure, it was unbearable to Rumi, who, according to Sepahsalar, viewed Shams as his *axis mundi*, a living iman, or saint, who, though his spirituality was concealed from the sight of most ordinary persons, nonetheless was the driving force behind his era's spiritual life. Sultan Valad referred to Shams as "in effect the leader of all those who had established complete communion with God." His glory, Valad asserts, was "veiled even from those themselves veiled in the glory of God."

In the third book of the *Mathnawi*, Rumi describes the predicament of these hidden saints who offered so much to the mundane society, which in turn did not recognize their worth or understand them:

> Another party go [to and fro] exceedingly hidden: how should they become well-known to the people of externals?
>
> They possess all this [spiritual dominion], and [yet] no one's eye falls upon their sovereignty for one moment.[4]

Rumi goes on to observe that the miracles of the living imans are concealed from ordinary people because these special beings dwell in a divine sanctuary that few can enter. Moreover, as Rumi puts it, ordinary people do not understand that the six directions of the earth are filled with the bounty of God. He then counsels readers to "enter the fire [of ecstasy]" if a "generous man" invites them to do so; they should put aside mundane worries that such a fire might burn or hurt them.

There is a sense of resignation in these lines. When Rumi warns the reader not to reject "the generous man"—quite possibly a reference to Shams—one senses that he knows quite well that many foolish people would reject such a man. In any case, for Rumi the loss of the *axis mundi* of his time was deeply unsettling and not something he could accept. Rumi either would have to find and bring back this living saint to Konya yet again, or find a new spiritual companion.

Some scholars believe that Rumi began writing his famous short verse couplets known as "ghazals" during this period, but Sultan Valad wrote that his father did not do so until a few years later. Then again there are some historians who believe Rumi may actually have written scattered verses before meeting Shams. However, literary convention has it that Rumi actualized his poetic talent only through encountering Shams.

Whatever the chronology of Rumi's poetic outpouring, a great many of his verses concern his deep anguish on learning of the loss of Shams. Much of his finest poetry seems to result from the almost unbearable combination of his overwhelming longing for Shams and the deep mystical awareness he cultivated under Shams' direction. Rumi's misery, shock and mystical depth all congealed in his overwhelming lyrical outburst.

Throughout the remainder of his life he was to frequently dedicate his remarkable powers of language to exploring the depths of his pain on losing Shams. Many lines in the *Mathnawi*, including ones which do not directly refer to Shams by name, take as their subject the agony of separation; it is as if this acute awareness of loss forms a sort of ever-present subtext. In some passages, the missing lover is a clear metaphor for the concept of Allah, in other cases the reader is more struck by a feeling of overwhelming longing for another human being.

In the "Tale of The Unworthy Lover," also in the third book of the *Mathnawi*, Rumi describes a world of "divine jealousy" in which all inhabitants apparently conspire to thwart a young man from seeing his love, a predicament with obvious parallels to the poet's unlucky relationship with Shams. Whenever the young man would send a message to his love through a messenger, the messenger would turn into a highwayman and bar the message from being delivered; if a letter should reach the woman, her secretary would read it aloud incorrectly, so that its meaning was lost. However, this intense suffering has a spiritual purpose; it enables the lovestruck youth to "break the banner of the army of cogitation," and approach an ecstatic understanding of God. Rumi explains: "The [Divine] jealousy barred [all] the ways of device and broke the banner of the army of cogitation."

FOR A LONG TIME Rumi heard nothing about Shams' whereabouts. Then one day, to his immense pleasure, he received a letter from the dervish sent from Syria; Rumi sent four letters in reply, but not all of these were answered. Later Rumi called for his trusted son, Sultan Valad, and dispatched him to Syria to visit Shams and beg him to return to Konya. In the *Divan-e* the poet describes his eagerness for the return of the Friend: "Bring me back that flighty idol by means of sweet songs, with golden excuses draft that fair moon so sweet to me back to this house." Rumi sent with his son a message containing an apology for the treachery of his zealous followers. Afzal Iqbal tells us that Rumi did not ask the Friend to come back to Konya until he had received assurances from the most devious disciples that they would not menace Shams again.

According to the hagiographers, factions had been develop-ing within the ranks of Rumi's followers since Shams first appeared on the scene. Not all the disciples had been disloyal; some had respected Rumi's bond with Shams. But there was considerable tension between the steadfast followers, who sympathetically shared Rumi's unhappiness, and the faithless students. This polarization heightened the mood of tension and sense of danger surrounding the relationship. During the time after Shams' removal, Rumi apparently expressed his outrage to the most treacherous of his disciples. Many of his followers went to Rumi numerous times to make apologies, but their teacher at first remained unforgiving and in a distraught state.

The account given by Sepahsalar describes how some of the crafty disciples, understanding that they had alienated Rumi, realized that they needed to regain his favor. The hagiographer says that in order to please Rumi, some of these people even gave silver and gold coins to Sultan Valad to take to Shams in Syria as tokens of apology. Sepahsalar describes Shams, upon learning of the coins, as laughing sweetly and then saying: "Why do you try to bribe me with gold and silver? The request of our master, so like Mohammad in character, is enough. How could I transgress his word and suggestion?" According to Sultan Valad's account, he entered Syria and relayed Rumi's messages to Shams; the dervish agreed to the request, and then he and Rumi's son held sama together joyfully for several days, before journeying back to Konya.

Nonetheless, some of the hagiographers depict Shams as having some reticence to return to the town where he was treated so nastily. By some accounts, Rumi sent many letters to Shams when he was in Damascus, but only a few were answered. There also is a legend that Sultan Valad discovered Shams playing chess in a caravansary in Damascus and that Shams initially responded in a lukewarm fashion to the young man's presence.

However the union was arranged or came about, the return took place sometime in 1247. Sultan Valad reports, in a gesture of theatrical humility, he walked all the way back, as Shams rode on a horse. As Sultan Valad later observed: "How could the servant ride in the presence of such a king?" A lavish welcome for the two men as they triumphantly enter Konya is also described by Sultan Valad; this by the same city which quite recently had all but expelled the dervish. According to Rumi's son, Rumi and all the other dignitaries of the city rushed out to greet Shams. Sultan Valad and Shams later joined Rumi and other family members and disciples for several days of joyful sama, with the ecstatic Rumi seated at Shams' side.

With the initial period after Shams' return, a degree of peacefulness prevailed between him and Rumi's disciples. Under Rumi's direction, many disciples offered apologies to Shams, and the dervish appeared to forgive them. However, Franklin Lewis suggests that Shams understood fully that these apologies were far from sincere. During this brief, happy respite, a relieved Rumi apparently began in earnest again his musical meditations. Sepahsalar tells us that in the winter of 1247, Shams asked Rumi for permission to marry Rumi's adopted daughter, a pretty, delicate young girl named Kimia, who, although apparently unrelated to the poet, had been raised in Rumi's household. Rumi was glad to grant his permission to a marriage that would, in effect, make Shams his son-in-law, thus fortifying the Friend's position in the household.

Unfortunately, not too long after Shams returned to Konya, the bitter jealousies were revived. According to Afzal Iqbal, one of the principal reasons Shams was detested by the status-loving students was that, under his influence, Rumi gave up his professorial gown to dress the part of the dervish.

Iqbal also traces some of the animosity to a widespread perception that Shams did not follow the Islamic tenets. In addition, there were some objections to his choice of words at times. A superficial observer of Shams might wrongly conclude that he did not concern himself with the basics of the Islamic faith. Given Rumi's spiritual attainments, it seemed to such people that his choice of

Shams as a companion was evidence of madness, especially the poet's frequent pronouncements that Shams was his "master."

Interestingly, in the *Maqalat* Shams reveals that he was well aware that there might have to be another separation, but nowhere does he describe the jealous disciples as the reason he might have to leave again. Shams shows himself to be touchingly concerned with Rumi's development and not at all focused on the possible impact that a new separation would have on him. Here one gets the sense that, for Shams, little existed—or at least mattered—beyond his own illumination and his efforts to transfer it to Rumi. He was able to write:

> It would be good if you [Rumi] can manage it so that I don't need to go away for the sake of your development, that this one journey I've made [to Syria] would suffice to reform you. I'm not in the position to order you to go on a journey, so it is I who will be obliged to go away for the sake of your development, for separation makes a person wise.[5]

Shams also declares that he would go away "fifty times," if necessary, if it would enable Rumi to advance. He adds that, beyond his concern for Rumi he does not much care whether he is in Anatolia or Syria.

RUMI WAS HEARTSICK that the disciples once again were disparaging his Beloved. The two men once more were spending long hours in each other's company, but Rumi also spent time with the disciples, and was especially attentive to those who had not plotted against Shams. Sultan Valad recalls that in one lecture Rumi bewailed the fact that he had no way to convince his weakest disciples of Shams' exalted spiritual station or worthiness of love. Many of the treacherous disciples, including those who recently had recanted and called Shams their *axis mundi*, once more reversed themselves and jealously attacked him. In this lecture Sultan Valad quotes his father saying mournfully, "No lover can tell anyone the reason for the goodness of his beloved, nor can any sign be planted in the heart of the lover that would point towards the hatefulness of the beloved."

Rumi later wrote quite a poignant verse to describe his dread during this period that he would once again have to endure a separation from Shams. He also reveals a jealous fear that some new friend would replace him in Shams' heart, and warns him to honor a "compact" between the two men. In the *Divan-e* Rumi writes:

> I heard that you intend traveling, don't.
> Nor bestow your love on any new friend.
> Though in this world you feel strange, know you've never
>   been estranged;
> Whatever pain you hope to wreak upon yourself: try not.
> Don't steal away from me, or seek out foreigners; Glancing
>   stealthily at another is also useless.[6]

By most accounts, Shams had an even more lethal enemy in Konya than Rumi's jealous, snide disciples: Ala al-Din, Rumi's younger son by his first wife, bitterly loathed Shams. This nasty relationship was in marked contrast to Shams' strong rapport with Sultan Valad, whom Shams educated and cherished, and who returned Shams' love. Sadly for Rumi, his oldest sons were as factionalized as his other disciples, with Sultan Valad firmly in the camp of the loyalists, while Ala al-Din was one of the leaders of the dissident faction.

There are several intriguing theories as to the source of Ala al-Din's deep hatred for Shams. Some writers have suggested that Ala al-Din had expected in some manner or time frame to become the successor of Rumi. The appointment of Shams as a kind of deputy, and the all-consuming love between the two men, may have seemed to Ala al-Din to dash or at least diminish his own prospects. Sultan Valad later wrote that some groups of Rumi's followers spread rumors that Shams had dislodged Ala al-Din from his father's affections. According to Sultan Valad, Shams was aware of the gossip.

The historian Golpinarli suggests an even more personal reason for the hatred: Ala al-Din may have been in love with Shams' young bride Kimia, who did not live long after their marriage. Apparently, she went out for an unchaperoned walk in a garden, caught some sort of illness there, and was dead within days. Within a week of her death, Shams traveled briefly to Damascus. Golpinarli suggests that Ala al-Din secretly loved Kimia and blamed Shams for allowing her to take the unchaperoned walk that led to her death. Of course, if Ala al-Din indeed loved this girl, he also must have resented the fact that Rumi selected the elderly Shams, rather than his own son, to be this young lady's husband in the first place. Other hagiographers note that during Shams' and Kimia's brief marriage, they occupied a small room in Rumi's house. On one occasion Ala al-Din purportedly passed by the couple's room and received a stern warning from Shams.

Franklin Lewis brands the theory that Shams and Ala al-Din were rivals in love as "extremely speculative," and that may well be true. Yet on a psychological and dramatic level this theory would explain the extremity of Ala al-Din's hatred of Shams. Kimia's death did, in any case, intensify many disciples' dislike of Shams, as did Rumi's continued preference for his company. There was a growing sense that once more Shams would have to depart Konya, and this quickly came to pass.

How—and if—Shams left Konya is an old and unsolved mystery; many, but not all, historians believe he was murdered.

Some believe a killing took place outside Rumi's own house.

Aflaki and Golpinarli both subscribe to the murder theory. Aflaki tells two variations of how the murder could have been committed. In the first Aflaki account, Rumi and Shams had been seated together in Rumi's house when someone knocked on the door. Quite melodramatically Shams announced to Rumi: "They are calling me to my murder." In this version, Shams stoically exits to face his killers. Seven of Rumi's evil disciples face Shams, and one stabs him to death.

In this first version from Aflaki, all seven of the evil disciples faint after the atrocity is committed. When they awake from their unconsciousness they find no corpse, only a few scattered drops of blood. Aflaki explains away the curious lack of a corpse by citing a witness's account that Shams managed to stagger away and die elsewhere. Aflaki attributed this first version to Sultan Valad, but Franklin Lewis notes that Sultan Valad himself never mentioned a murder in his own writings. But it is conceivable that a murder took place, and that Sultan Valad did no want to publicize widely a story that would reflect badly on his family. If so, he could have confided certain details to Aflaki in private. Aflaki could have chosen to make this story public, despite Sultan Valad's wishes.

Aflaki also relates a second variation of this murder tale in which the connivers tossed Shams' body down a well after his death; he attributes this story to Fateme Khatun, the wife of Sultan Valad. In this variation, the ghost of Shams pays a visit to Sultan Valad in a dream and tells him the location of the corpse. Then Sultan Valad, under the cover of night, gathers some close disciples and retrieves the body, perfumes it and reburies it in a hastily dug underground tomb on the grounds of the madrase where Rumi teaches.

Aflaki—never one to pass up a succulent tale—indicates that he believes this second version. He says he believes it because he learned it from his mentor Ulu Aref Chelebi, who was the son of Sultan Valad's wife, Fateme Khatun. Aflaki also claims that Rumi did not attend the funeral of Ala al-Din, who died fifteen years after the disappearance of Shams. He interprets Rumi's failure to attend the funeral as indicating that the poet learned of the murder, but long after the fact.

The historian Golpinarli also thought it likely that Sultan Valad—although hardly sympathetic to his murderous brother—engaged in a cover-up of a tale of a murder that could dishonor the entire Valad family. Golpinarli gives the date of the "martyrdom" of Shams as December 5, 1247. His theory is that the murder took place but was not discovered by Rumi until many years later because Sultan Valad and other relatives wanted to spare Rumi pain. Golpinarli reasons that when Rumi finally discovered the killing he chose to keep it a secret, and that Sultan Valad and Sepahsalar, following Rumi's example, did not write about the murder. Golpinarli believed that Rumi had a condemnatory verse inscribed on Ala al-Din's gravestone. However, for some enigmatic reason, he also concludes that Shams had forgiven Ala al-Din "from the other world."

At no point in his writing does Sultan Valad actually mention the possibility that Shams may have been murdered; he alludes only to a sudden disappearance. The modern historians Afzal Iqbal and Franklin Lewis both conclude that it is wisest to accept Sultan Valad's statement that Shams again disappeared suddenly, given that Sultan Valad was the authoritative biographer of Rumi in the poet's lifetime. Lewis is troubled by the perplexing lack of a corpse, noting, quite sensibly, that all murders require a body.

However, the Islamicist Annemarie Schimmel believes that such a corpse actually was dug up during a recent excavation near the grounds of Rumi's madrase in Konya, and that there is reason to believe it may be the remains of Shams. She also cites a verse from Rumi in which he appears to hint that he has intuited his Friend's death: "The earth is not dust, it is a vessel full of blood. From the blood of lovers, from the wound of checkmate."

In addition, Lewis also notes that Ala al-Din apparently left Konya after Shams' disappearance because of an inquiry into some sort of plot against Shams in which Ala al-Din was implicated for some unclear reason. Lewis cites letters from Rumi, urging his child to return and face the authorities. The letters address Ala al-Din tenderly, perhaps suggesting that the inquiry centered on a charge less serious than murder. Alternatively, Rumi may have been aware of charges of murder, but he may have believed that Ala al-Din was not guilty.

Lewis notes a truly fantastic version of the supposed murder of Shams told by Uzun Ferdowsi Deraz, a Turkish writer who around 1500 collected anecdotes from a Sufi school known as the Bektashi dervishes. This anecdote apparently was concocted to glorify the school and is beyond outlandish. Yet the fanciful nature of the story illustrates the strong hold that the legend of Shams' killing had on many imaginations.

In this dazzling tale, no less than Sultan Valad is the murderer—and not Ala al-Din. Sultan Valad commits the murder to restore family honor, after learning that there is gossip that his father, due to the evil influence of Shams, performs sama with women present. The vengeful Sultan Valad cuts off Shams' head, only to have Shams rise up in sama and dance toward Tabriz, bearing his own head. The besotted Rumi also mystically transports himself to Tabriz, in search of Shams. Once there, Rumi finds Shams dancing on top of a green minaret. Rumi dashes to the top of the minaret, to join his beloved. But Shams eludes him, running back down to the bottom of the minaret. Rumi darts down to the bottom, and Shams returns to the top. This ritual of levitational hide-and-seek is performed seven times. Finally, an exhausted Rumi throws himself off the top of the minaret and is caught in midair by Shams, who tells Rumi to bury him there. Shams also directs Rumi to pay his respects to the Bektashi Order.

Whether Shams was killed or whether he left Konya on his own accord, the sad fact remains that it had become impossible for Rumi to keep his Beloved at his side. It can be said that Rumi's own society, which rated the poet so highly, simply could not tolerate his immense love for the dervish, even after Rumi begged it to do so.

At the same time, it is possible that Shams left on his own accord, in order to spur Rumi to new spiritual heights through yet another separation. Or he could have left simply because he was a Sufi wanderer by habit and principle. But this wouldn't alter the fact that there were many plotting disciples who wanted him to leave. In either case, Rumi once more was plunged into despair and he blamed the disciples for the loss; the poet never once mentioned in his verses that Shams might have left on purpose to spur Rumi to new levels of spiritual mastery.

Although Afzal Iqbal stops short of concluding that a murder took place, he reports with assurance that news of Shams' death spread throughout Konya. According to Iqbal, the disconsolate Rumi heard these rumors, but refused to believe them. Later Rumi would write: "Who dared say that that immortal one met his death? Who dared say that the Sun of hope has set? Lo, an enemy of the Sun came up to the roof, Closed his two eyes and exclaimed the Sun had set!"[7]

AFTER THE DERVISH'S second disappearance, the heartbroken Rumi becomes desperate once more for news of Shams. Iqbal tells a story in which Rumi asks every traveler he meets, if they have seen Shams. One day a traveler told Rumi that he had seen

Shams in Damascus. Rumi was so happy that he took off his robe on the spot and gave it to the traveler. A friend later pointed out that the traveler may have lied to Rumi. Rumi, according to Iqbal, said: "Had I believed the news to be true, I would have given him my life and not my robe!" In his misery, he began to dedicate himself with increasing levels of fervor to music, the art form once forbidden to him which his beloved Shams had freed him to enjoy. His passion for music shocked many of his contemporaries, but Rumi, now firmly under Shams' influence didn't seem to mind the notoriety.

Sultan Valad describes his father during this phase as bewitched by music, unable to be without it for any length of time. He also tells us that Rumi, now a true dervish, had ceased to have any practical concerns about money or possessions. Sultan Valad writes: "Day and night he danced in ecstasy, On the earth he revolved like the Heavens. His [ecstatic] cries reached the zenith of the skies and were heard by all and sundry." He also tells us that his father lavished expensive gold and silver coins on musicians, losing all concern for material wealth. Rumi's only concerns were for music and ecstasy, which he could not bear to forego, even for a second.

Apparently, during this time, Rumi's entire personality underwent a metamorphosis; once the quintessence of professorial propriety and restraint, Rumi, perhaps sensing that he now was deprived of Shams forever, grew edgy, frenzied and wild. Afzal Iqbal describes the poet at this time as "living dangerously," noting that many of his contemporaries believed that Rumi had gone mad. And, by most accounts, Rumi was displaying definite signs of madness. But, at the same time, the renewed separation was having another interesting effect upon Rumi: miserable though he was, he also appears to have been energized in some strange way by his great loss.

Dance of the dervishes, Istanbul.
(Foto Marburg/Art Resource, NY)

The hagiographers tell us that the first time Shams left
Konya, Rumi withdrew into himself and could not enjoy music
much until Shams returned to Konya. But after Shams' second
disappearance, there emerged a wretched but somehow embold-
ened Rumi, a defiant lover of sama, a man more angry than
depressed. This is the Rumi that flaunted his love of music
before the good citizens of Konya. Here we find a Sufi who was
quite willing to defy convention to pursue his own, higher
truths. Here we encounter, at long last, a free man, albeit a
somewhat crazy one.

9

Mad for Music

Man craves winter in summer, and when winter comes, he likes it not,
For he is never content with any state [of things], neither with
poverty not with a life of plenty. May man be killed! How ungrateful
he is! Whenever he obtains guidance, he spurns it.[1]

—*Jalalu'ddin Rumi*

MAY MAN BE KILLED INDEED! It's difficult not to draw parallels
between the foolish people of Saba described in these bitterly
ironic verses from the third book of the *Mathnawi* and Rumi's
scheming disciples, the ungrateful, shortsighted citizens of
Konya. During the immediate aftermath of Shams' second and
final departure, Rumi was completely alienated from many of his
former associates, shunning those who had, in effect, refused the
"kindness" of Shams' illumination and "spurned his guidance."
Drawing close to a few trusted followers and relatives, he delved
obsessively into the practice of sama. The frantic, sorrowful poet
found solace chiefly in music, although he probably also began
composing his verses at this time.

It still would be years before he would summon the emotional stamina to compose his masterwork, the *Mathnawi*, a
sprawling six-book masterpiece more than twice the length of
that other equally famous medieval work, Dante's *Divine
Comedy*. But, in the wake of Shams' leaving, Rumi took to composing the short-form "ghazals," or lyrical poems that make up
the *Divan-e*. A few literary historians date some of these poems

to Shams' first departure, while others claim they were all written after his second disappearance.

Many of these relatively early verses lack the breadth and sweeping quality of the *Mathnawi*, but they display a brilliant grasp of poetic metrics and are incisively focused and deeply affecting in their emotional rawness. In one sense, the *Divan-e* comprises a record of Rumi's misery after Shams' departure. In an early ghazal Rumi addresses Shams, describing how he has deteriorated after Shams' disappearance:

> Know that with your departure my mind and faith have been
> stripped.
> This poor heart of mine no longer has patience or resolve.
> Don't ask me about my wan face, my troubled heart, or the
> burning in my soul.
> See with your own eyes, no power of words can explain these
> things.[2]

Composing the intensely rhythmical ghazals of the *Divan-e* appears to have had a stabilizing impact on Rumi, much like the solace he found in mystic twirling. Many critics have noted Rumi's ability to 'play' language almost as if it were musical notes. There is reason to think that he drew on his musical sense as a sort of emotional balm during his period of crisis, as he alternated between extremes of pain and composure. In many of Rumi's ghazals there is an odd tension between frightening and comforting images. Rumi at times serves up unsettling phrases that describe his emotional upheaval, then follows them immediately with select blocks of soothing words, quite likely arranged to numb his own pain.

The critic Fatemeh Keshavarz writes that: "Rumi demonstrates an awareness of symmetry as a stabilizing factor in the

The sacred whirling, a religious ritual of the Sufis,
called "sama," performed here by
contemporary dervishes in Istanbul.

frenzied moments of love. When things seem to be getting out of control because simple linguistic conventions and elaborate rules of prosody have been overlooked, a sense of symmetry defies chaos and replaces the lost order."[3]

One of the most intriguing features of the *Divan-e* is that Rumi signed this collection of odes "Shams al-Din of Tabriz," as if Shams had written them, signifying the poet's sense of oneness with the dervish, and also suggesting that the person who inspired so many of these odes was also on some serious level the author of the work. Here we find a suggestion that Rumi and Shams were practically interchangeable. The conventional Western and modern distinctions between subject and object, and writer and protagonist don't apply here. We have, instead, a kind of literary and spiritual fusion of identity, as if the unstrung Rumi does not think it very important to distinguish between himself and the man who left him in his mournful state.

During this period after his Beloved's final leaving, Rumi was extremely unstable, unsteadied by both the loss of Shams and the major changes that had taken place in his own psyche under Shams' tutelage. During his brief few years with Shams, Rumi eschewed academic knowledge for intuitive wisdom and was forced to reconfigure his personality and role in society. He had not completely abandoned his duties at the madrase, but he was functioning there in an eccentric manner: much of the time when he might have been teaching, he instead was absorbed in ecstatic dance.

There are many suggestions that Rumi spent a good number of years struggling to retain his sanity in the wake of Shams' final departure. Afzal Iqbal writes: "Although the fire and the fury of the storm had appreciably subsided by 1250, Rumi had yet to take years before he could settle down in a state in which he could recollect the intense emotional experience of this era without causing a serious emotional breakdown in his own personality." It also would take years before Rumi would come to terms with the fact that he was never to see Shams alive again. In truth, he was to live a full twenty years after Shams' second disappearance, but it would be quite some time before he could make sense of this loss. Rumi, for many months, did not give up on the prospect of finding his Beloved and reuniting with him once more. Some of the ghazals in the *Divan-e* hint that Rumi believed Shams to be either in Syria, or to have gone back to Tabriz in Iran. In one such ghazal in the *Divan-e*, Rumi wrote:

Strange, where did that gorgeous heartbreaker go?
Odd, where'd that tall supple cypress go?
He bathed us like a candle in his light; in thin air vanished,
   left us! Where'd he go?
My heart, leaf-like, trembles all day long at this:
Where'd, at midnight, all alone, that heartthrob go?[4]

Through 1247 and much of 1248, Rumi apparently believed that Shams was still alive; some historians have guessed that he could have received a letter from Shams. Sometime in 1247, or perhaps in early 1248, Rumi gathered a few trusted disciples and went to Damascus in search of Shams. There are descriptions from some of the hagiographers of the people of Damascus appearing stunned to see a man of the poet's attainments seeking an obscure person; no one in Damascus had even noticed Shams or knew who he was, according to these stories.

The search party returned without success to Konya after several months, according to Sultan Valad. Rumi some months later organized a second journey to Syria to search for Shams; this trip was longer than the first but also turned up no trace of the dervish. By some accounts, there were a few other such search parties, but the record is sketchy here. Whether there really were additional journeys to find Shams or not, Rumi clearly was unwilling to give up easily on the possibility that his Beloved might be located. Franklin Lewis concludes that it wasn't until 1250 that Rumi lost all hope of seeing Shams again, and began in earnest the business of finding a way to live without the dervish. Rumi's poetic efforts to impart to the world his sadness and the strange and profound truths he had learned from Shams were to provide him with a purpose in life.

As for Shams—there is no real way to know what happened to him after he left Rumi's home. If he wasn't murdered, he could have gone on to live many more years and to wander much more throughout the Islamic world in his quiet, undetected manner. However, many historians believe that Shams was not murdered and left Konya alive, but was to live only a few months or years longer; these historians hypothesize that Rumi's resignation to Shams' death, which seems to have set in around 1250, may well have been a response to receiving a piece of solid information that the dervish had died.

The location of Shams' remains, if indeed there are such remains, also is a mystery; yet the lack of a tomb or other monument would be thoroughly in keeping with Shams' modest, hermetic ways. Various cities in Turkey, Iran and Pakistan have staked claims to being the dervish's final resting place, but there is no consensus of opinion among historians about these claims. And it is hard not to wonder if Shams, a man given to secrecy and bored with convention, would not have been happy to know that in death he was once more unlocatable.

IF SHAMS LEFT KONYA alive and lived a long or short while longer, there is good reason to conjecture he would have done so in good spirits. Shams was a man who had spent decades wandering alone, a person who almost automatically rejected most teachers, scholars, jurists and dervishes as insufferably vacuous. One might even be tempted to call Shams a bit of a spiritual snob, given his vast preference for his own company over that of most other people, including his own father. Surely another period of solo wandering would not have been unpleasant to him. He, unlike Rumi, was unlikely to play the role of the lonely, dejected lover to the hilt.

From his own writings, we learn that, though thoroughly enamored of Rumi, Shams at the same time also was strangely independent and untroubled by separation from the poet. He wrote in the *Maqalat* of his original separation from Rumi: "If truly you cannot accompany me, I do not care. I was not bothered by separation from Mowlana [Rumi], nor does union with him bring me pleasure. My pleasure comes from within me and my suffering comes from within me. Now, living with me is difficult."[5]

This passage reveals one of the most remarkable facets of Shams' character: his complete self-reliance. A wanderer who spent the better part of his life searching for someone of Rumi's caliber, Shams had been overjoyed to encounter such an individual as Rumi at long last. And yet—in intriguing contrast to the heartsick Rumi—Shams was not especially perturbed at the prospect of losing him just a few short years later. The reclusive Shams remained absolutely self-contained, loving Rumi but not needing him, secure in the knowledge that he was the author of his own misery and joy.

In time Rumi was to calm down, comforted by the knowledge that he, too, like Shams, had internalized the essence of their unique friendship. Through his poetry, Rumi began to manifest in verse the mystic lessons he had learned from Shams. Sultan Valad in his writings describes his father as having arrived

Dervishes Burst Into 'Sacred Whirling' of Sama

Aflaki tells us that *sama* or "sacred whirling," and music came to be as important to Rumi as formal prayer. One day Rumi was in a state of rapture as he listened to a friend play the violin. He was interrupted by another friend, summoning him to afternoon prayer. But Rumi refused to accompany his second friend to afternoon prayers, explaining that both music and prayers "speak" to God, who wants formal prayers, "for his service," and music for the sake of love and knowledge. Rumi went on to add, somewhat enigmatically, that there is a secret hidden in the depths of music, which cannot be revealed because it would "upset the world," according to Aflaki.

During Rumi's lifetime the dance of *sama* was performed spontaneously, often alongside food and drink. According to Aflaki, Rumi and his fellow dervishes frequently would burst into the twirling dance in the streets of Konya, sometimes after returning from an evening prayer service. There are many verses praising the joys of *sama* and the feelings of natural harmony produced by it in *The Mathnawi*. In Book III, Rumi writes that when musicians strike their tambourines they produce such a strong state of ecstasy that "the seas burst into foam."

The sacred whirling of the Mevlevi Order is still performed today and is an imitation of the order of the cosmos, revealed by the rotations of the planets. Some scholars associate this twirling with Pythagoras' theory of the "music of the spheres," which states that the movement of the heavenly bodies throughout the universe is determined by the laws of harmony. The *sama* ceremony performed by the Mevlevi Order today is performed in a highly ritualized manner, according to a specific arrangement set down in the seventeenth century. The ceremony commemorates Rumi's' own death, an event he always looked forward to and described in joyous terms. Novice members of the Mevlevi Order today learn to twirl by spinning around a large nail placed next to the big nail of the left foot.

The dance in its current form

begins with a flautist playing a "ney," or reed flute. Dancers enter dressed to resemble an elegant tomb not unlike the one that Rumi was buried in. The dancers wear white robes to symbolize the funeral shroud, large black coats, which represent the tomb, and very tall hats, which signify the tombstone. Finally, a sheikh, or spiritual leader, enters last and salutes the other dervishes. They salute in return as the sheikh sits down on a bright red carpet which is viewed as a symbol of a brilliant crimson sunset—a reference to the beauty of the evening sky on the night Rumi passed away. The sheikh begins to sing praises of the Prophet Mohammad written by Rumi and music written by a late seventeenth-century Turkish composer and member of the Mevlevi Order named Itri.

The flautist begins to improvise a bit, and a kettle-drums player also begins to perform improvisationally, while the sheik knocks on the ground. The dervishes advance slowly and perform three slow turns. These turns also are highly symbolic and represent three paths which bring men to God. They are the paths of science, vision and union with God. At the end of the third turn the skeikh returns to the carpet and the dancers remove their coats in yet another symbolic gesture: signifying the casting off of the tomb in order to experience a second birth. When the sheikh grants the dancers permission to dance, they begin to move about very slowly in rotational movements like those of the planets around the sun. When the performance is nearly over, the sheikh stands and quickens the rhythm of the music. At the conclusion there is a musical finale and a recitation of prayers from the Koran.

Troupes of dervishes regularly perform the *sama* in public auditoriums in Europe and the United States. Although many of the movements of the dancers are achingly slow, audiences consistently say that they find these performances fascinating. The intense concentration and sincerity of the dervishes gives their ponderous and deliberate movements a nearly hypnotic quality. At the end of such performances, audiences are asked not to clap as the *sama* is a religious ritual, not an entertainment.

at an understanding that he had fused with Shams in his heart and that he no longer needed to search for Shams. "He [Rumi] said: 'Since I'm him, for what do I search? I'm his mirror image and will speak myself,'" Sultan Valad reflects.

In one of his ghazals, Rumi discusses the impossibility of locating Shams physically, and his dawning realization that he would only be able to encounter his Beloved inside his own heart:

> I questioned Ibn Sina about his condition; he transcended even his worthy intellect.
> I journeyed to the place of two bow-lengths; He was not in that exalted court.
> Then I gazed into my own heart where I saw Him; He was nowhere else.
> Except pure-hearted Shams, Wild One, none ever attained his drunkenness or anguish.[6]

After Rumi came to terms with his loss of Shams, he took another spiritual companion, a goldsmith in Konya named Salah al-Din Zarkob. Due to his belief in the need for an *axis mundi* Rumi required the special spiritual companionship of a living iman or saint. He could not have contented himself with memories of Shams.

Again the poet's choice of preferred companion was to infuriate much of the ulema of Konya. Although having had studied with the same mentor as Rumi—Borhan al-Din Mohaqqeq—Salah al-Din was considered quite ignorant by other residents of Konya. And in truth, Salah al-Din left no surviving writings to establish any sort of intellectual credentials. However, his teacher Borhan al-Din Mohaqqeq, as was his tendency, was believed to have stressed the importance of fasting and other purification rituals over intellectuality to this student.

The renewed outrage of some members of the ulema at Rumi's taste in companions was curious in some ways. Even though Rumi had been steadfast in his loyalty to his previous Beloved, Shams, there is an odd sense that the citizens of Konya may have expected him to abandon his dervish dress and return to his staid, professorial ways of old after Shams' leaving. They certainly were stunned by his new affection for Salah al-Din, who was rumored to be dimmer even than the supposedly imbecilic Shams. But this criticism was irrelevant to Rumi, who was taken with his new companion's gentleness and mystical ways.

Once more, Rumi was not influenced by the gossip, immersing himself in the company of his new Beloved and writing verses for him. In all, Rumi was to dedicate seventy-one ghazals to Salah al-Din. In one such verse he writes about his new friend as if he were his sheikh, describing him in terms one would reserve for a distant but compassionate master who teaches a complex lesson through harsh means. In this ghazal Rumi plays the role of the student, and also writes contemptuously of those who can't fathom Salah al-Din's beauty:

I replied: "You're harsh, like such a one." "Know," he said, "it's for your own good, not because of anger or spite."
Whoever enters saying, "It's me," hit him on the head; this is the shrine of love, fool! It's not a sheep-pen.
Surely, Salah al-Din is the image of the perfect beauty; wipe your eyes, see for yourself this rare image of the heart.[7]

Although Rumi displayed the same dedication to his new Beloved as he had to Shams—bestowing on him such elaborate terms of endearment as "the image of perfect beauty" and "rare image of the heart"—his two companions were quite different in temperament. Where the intense Shams had a volcanic effect on

Rumi, Salah al-Din was gentle and soothing; Salah al-Din's calming ways probably helped Rumi recover from the emotional jolts he underwent during his years with Shams.

The hagiographers record an appealing tale about the manner in which Rumi came to realize Salah al-Din would be his new companion. During one of the poet's fits of dancing in the streets of Konya, he was distracted by a rhythmical, pounding sound. The sound proved to come from the beating of the goldsmith's hammer as he fashioned a piece of silver. Completely charmed, Rumi lingered in front of the goldsmith's shop in a state of ecstasy. In deference to Rumi, the humble goldsmith kept pounding at the piece of silver until there was nothing left of it, so that Rumi might continue to enjoy the sound. Rumi later wrote: "I discovered a treasure in the shop of a gold leaf maker. What a form, what a content, what a beauty, what a grace."

Another colorful version of their initial meeting is provided by Sepahsalar. In this tale Salah al-Din heard Rumi preach, and was thrilled to hear him repeat many of the points that their shared mentor Borhan al-Din had made during his lifetime. According to Sepahsalar, Salah al-Din, upon hearing such a speech, ran up and kissed the feet of Rumi.

Sultan Valad at times wrote sympathetically about Salah al-Din's role in his father's life, noting that the goldsmith was only trying to provide the poet with a mirror. "They are offended that the Mowlana [Rumi] has singled me out for his favors," said Valad, once summarizing the goldsmith's words to criticisms of himself. "But," the goldsmith had continued, "they know not that I am but a mirror. The mirror does not reflect itself [but the one who looks into it.] In me he sees himself; [t]hen why should he not choose to see himself?"[8] Other historians have explained Rumi's choice of Salah al-Din by noting that the goldsmith apparently possessed a mystical fervor that entranced Rumi. The two men's shared mentor, Borhan al-Din Mohaqqeq, allegedly once said he had bequeathed his eloquence to Rumi and his mystical gifts to Salah al-Din.

WHEN RUMI BEGAN his ardent relationship with Salah al-Din, both men were mature. This prevented a conventional mentor-disciple relationship, as had been the case with Rumi and Shams. These two men also were equals, or spiritual companions. Afzal Iqbal referred to Salah al-Din as Rumi's "alter ego and confidant," in another example of the unique way in which Rumi's identity commingled with that of his Beloveds.

Rumi appointed his new friend as his deputy at the madrase and told the disciples to treat Salah al-Din as their sheikh. Once again the selection of a deputy outside the family was to threaten the peace of Rumi's household, but this time the chagrined party was Rumi's favorite child, the compliant Sultan Valad, not the treacherous Ala al-Din. Although Sultan Valad was to remain obedient to Rumi and Salah al-Din, there are indications he had to struggle to accept his father's new choice of companion and deputy and the surrounding controversy.

It was common enough for professors in madrases to appoint deputies to assist them in their teaching duties if they had to hold multiple sessions, according to Franklin Lewis. However, there was little precedent in a reputable madrase for the selection of a relatively uneducated goldsmith. This appointment reinforced the widespread impression that Rumi and his entourage were functioning in an abnormal manner. In truth, Rumi had given up many of the trappings of conventionality quite some time earlier. But it seems that some of the disciples had never brought themselves to accept this state of affairs. Once more, there was bitterness among the disciples who felt excluded and, once more, Rumi was to side with the companion, not his students.

On one occasion when Salah al-Din was criticized by others at the madrase, Rumi rushed to his defense, mentioning that Salah was humble, and always deferred to Rumi. Yet Rumi had effectively made Salah al-Din, his sheikh: a move that only heightened the ambivalence surrounding the relationship. The very equality of the friendship, and the confusion surrounding the issue of who was the master and who was the disciple, made it even more controversial and threatening to jealous disciples.

By this time, the eloquent and well-educated Sultan Valad had begun to make an impression with his speaking. Before Salah al-Din's arrival, there may have been speculation that he would be appointed his father's successor in much the manner that Rumi had followed Baha al-Din. There also may have been attempts by some disciples to have Sultan Valad installed as his father's successor, in part because of his excellence as a speaker, and in part because he might have proven more helpful in securing audiences with Rumi for the disciples, according to Franklin Lewis.

Quite fascinatingly, Sultan Valad, who never once remarked, even hinted, in his writings at the possibility of Shams' having been killed, wrote about plotters who allegedly wished to murder and bury Salah al-Din. According to Sultan Valad's account, a sincere disciple came and revealed the scheme, and Salah al-Din laughing, explained, "no straw could move, unless God willed it."

Rumi was infuriated when he learned of the plot against his new Beloved. He ostracized the alleged authors of the scheme and withdrew into the exclusive company of the goldsmith. The plotting disciples apparently had learned nothing from the history of Rumi's relationship to Shams, and foolishly had not foreseen their ostracization. They began to weep and plead for forgiveness, which Rumi and Salah al-Din, at length, granted to them. Rumi in his *Discourses* praised Salah al-Din highly and chastised those who rejected him, proclaiming that men for centuries have abandoned their homes and families and searched the world for a person of his caliber. Yet those who encountered Salah al-Din in Konya abandoned him, an irony Rumi could not fathom.

It appears possible that the polished and competent Sultan Valad for a time resented the influence of the less cultivated Salah al-Din within Rumi's circle. At one point, Sultan Valad appears to have struggled with a demand from Salah al-Din that he hand over a sermon he wrote and allow Salah al-Din to deliver it in public. Yet, Sultan Valad later concluded that giving up his public speaking had been an exercise in humility and that he had benefited from it. At any rate, it's worth noting that Rumi, who was from childhood the unquestioned successor of his own father, preferred to select his deputies and companions from outside the family. With his unconventional choices, the poet was to stir up ill feelings, not just among his disciples but also within his own family. It is hard not to wonder if Rumi ever pondered the large discrepancy between his evidently harmonious relationship with the long-suffering Baha al-Din, and his more charged relations with his comparatively privileged sons.

DESPITE THE INITIAL STRUGGLES Sultan Valad endured with Salah al-Din, this relationship never approached the pitch of animosity that existed between Shams and Ala al-Din. Rumi demanded that Sultan Valad follow Salah al-Din as his spiritual master, and his dutiful son in time agreed. Later, Salah al-Din w to ask Sultan Valad to accept him with his "heart and soul,"

Sultan Valad agreed to do so. But still there were indications he did not cherish this new mentor to the extent he had Shams.

Adding to the uneasy situation, Rumi arranged for Sultan Valad to marry Fateme Khatun, the daughter of Salah al-Din. Afzal Iqbal suggests that Rumi may have arranged this marriage in order to solidify Salah al-Din's role in his household and make it harder for the jealous disciples to separate the two men. According to Aflaki, Rumi had known this girl since she was a small child and had taught her to read the Koran. The poet evidently thought more highly of Fateme Khatun than any of his other female disciples. Sepahsalar refers to Fateme Khatun as a "female saint on earth," and indicates that as a child she also spent some time with her father Salah al-Din in the presence of his teacher Borhan al-Din.

Unfortunately, Sultan Valad does not appear to have joined in this widespread admiration for his wife. Possibly he resented the marriage for reinforcing his subordinate position to Salah al-Din, who was now both his sheikh and his father-in-law. Then again, he may have expected to marry a woman of more elevated status than this daughter of a simple goldsmith.

After the marriage, Rumi wrote a letter to the young woman, assuring her that he would not allow Sultan Valad to insult her and telling her that she was not guilty of any offense. "If my dear son strives to hurt you, I shall verily verily take away my love from him. I will give up loving him. I shall not respond to his greetings. I do not want him to come to my funeral," says Rumi.[7] At the same time, he also wrote a conciliatory letter to Sultan Valad, assuring him that neither he nor Fateme would intrude in his affairs. He showed his devotion to another daughter of Salah al-Din, Hadiyya Khatun, by using his wealthy connections to help secure an impressive dowry for her on the occasion of her marriage to a calligrapher.

Rumi was to keep company with Salah al-Din for ten years. Although the relationship generated its share of controversy, including the apparent murder plot, the outrage did not reach the levels of intensity created by Rumi's association with Shams; Salah al-Din was not forced out of Konya. Still, there is a sense that Rumi's circle was permeated by a very odd and dangerous type of jealousy and that to be the Beloved of the poet was an unsafe occupation. Rumi, in his writings, left few clues as to how he felt about being the object of such remarkably intense and bitter rivalries; it is not easy to say whether he ever reflected on the odd phenomenon of his astonishing popularity and the primitive feelings of jealousy he inspired. However, in his life he seems to have sided always with his Beloveds when rivalries and plots arose.

Despite such intrigues, Salah al-Din was able to live safely in Konya as Rumi's special spiritual companion for about ten years, before suffering a serious illness. The illness apparently was protracted; during this time Rumi abandoned his daily affairs to nurse his friend. When Salah al-Din passed away, he left the request that his funeral be celebrated with sama and he invited the dervishes to dance on his grave. At that time the use of music remained a controversial subject in Islamic music, and Rumi's circle was considered blasphemous by some for embracing sama. Quite likely the inclusion of music in a funeral procession struck some Konya residents as a new low in the circle's profane cavortings.

Following his death, Rumi composed these lines in memory of Salah al-Din: "O, Salah al-Din! You have gone, you fast-flying homa-bird—You have leapt from the bow like an arrow—and that bow has wept."[10]

AFTER THE DEATH OF Salah al-Din, Rumi was to choose a th' and final spiritual companion, Hosam al-Din Chelebi. Afla' described Hosam al-Din as appealing, gentle and kind and able to attract converts to Islam. Sepahsalar said that this special friend was so empathetic that whenever someone near him suffered a pain he would experience it also. After years of acquaintence, Rumi appointed Hosam al-Din as his sheikh; and Hosam demonstrated devotion to Rumi by voluntarily taking care of his financial matters.

This new friend was a native of Konya and had grown up in an Islamic fraternal lodge that was a sort of variant on the Sufi lodges. While Hosam al-Din was still a teenager, his father, the leader of the lodge, passed away. By legend, the other members of the lodge turned to the young Hosam al-Din and asked him to be their new leader. However, he allegedly refused and led the entire fraternity to Rumi. In the manner of Shams and Rumi, Hosam al-Din was fastidious on the subject of following the Prophet closely. An anecdote from Aflaki suggests that, once again, Rumi's preferred friend was not taken seriously by the ulema. In this story, Rumi was invited somewhere to give a speech, but declined to do so until Hosam al-Din also was invited to speak. When Hosam finally arrived, Rumi rushed to greet him, saying, "Welcome my spirit, my faith."

Appointing Hosam al-Din as his new deputy, Rumi instructed the disciples to consider him their sheikh. Although there appear to have been some doubts about Hosam al Din's suitability, this time the disciples accepted him; it seems Rumi's students finally had grasped that they had no power to separate Rumi from his Beloveds. Despite some grumbling about Hosam al-Din's qualifications, there is no evidence that serious plots against him were ever contemplated. There is a suggestion in Aflaki's writings that Rumi's relationship with his third and final companion may have been less intense than his all-consuming associations with Shams and Salah al-Din. Unlike these prior relationships, they did not spend all their time together. This is partly because the two men were separated for about two months of every year while Rumi, now advanced in years, visited a hot springs resort.

And yet the relationship in some ways was the most critical of all Rumi's special companionships because it provided him with the stability to produce his masterwork, the *Mathnawi*, which is dedicated to Hosam al-Din and which Rumi might not have been able to produce without his third and final Beloved. Rumi tells us that many subjects discussed in his epic-length poem were in fact Hosam al-Din's spiritual discoveries. While Shams and Salah al-Din may have provided tremendous sources of inspiration for Rumi's ghazals, Hosam al-Din's role in producing the *Mathnawi* was even more central: he appears to have been constantly present as Rumi labored away on it, involving himself as minutely as Rumi in the poetic process.

Scholars note that for more than a decade Hosam al-Din traveled virtually everywhere with Rumi. Taking down nearly every word as the master paid visits to houses, baths, lectures and ceremonies of sama. Once Rumi's words were transcribed, the good-natured Hosam would distribute copies to all the disciples. By legend, Hosam received the inspiration for the book itself at the same time that Rumi did, but independently of Rumi. According to the hagiographers, the two men discovered the strange coincidence while wandering together through vineyards outside Konya one day. Suddenly Hosam suggested that Rumi write a great book like those of Sana'i or Attar. More specifically, he encouraged Rumi to produce a unique and broad-ranging work that would be treasured by troubadours who could compose music to accompany its rhymes.

According to this fable, Rumi smiled and reached in

turban and produced a paper containing eighteen lines, the famous first lines of the *Mathnawi*, which, not surprisingly, took up the themes of passionate spiritual friendship, the agonies of separation, and the joys of union:

> Listen to the reed how it tells a tale, complaining of separations—Saying, "Ever since I was parted from the reed-bed, my lament hath caused man and woman to moan. I want a bosom torn by severance, that I may unfold [to such a one] the pain of love-desire. Every one who is left far from his source wishes back the time when he was united with it. In every company I uttered my wailful notes, I consorted with the unhappy and with them that rejoice. Every one became my friend from his own opinion; none sought out my secrets from within me."[11]

Rumi's special relationship with Hosam al-Din shaped the poet's masterwork to an unusual degree. Whether or not Rumi and Hosam actually both had the inspiration for the *Mathnawi* at the same time or not, the work is permeated with the influence of Hosam al-Din. The vulnerable, susceptible Rumi was oddly dependent on this friend, as he had been upon Shams and Salah al-Din—but in some ways to an even greater extent. Hosam was at some points the work's subject, at other times its muse, at other moments its reader, and on still other occasions its scribe.

ALTHOUGH RUMI SIGNED Shams' name to the *Divan-e*, this was really only a poetic touch. There was little likelihood that Shams produced many, or even any, of the ghazals. Yet in a very real sense, Hosam al-Din was the co-author of the *Mathnawi*. In both cases, Rumi's involvement of his Beloveds in the creation of his poetry was thorough. We find none of the modern notion of the isolated poet, secreted away somewhere as he labors over his verses in solitude. For Rumi, poetry was more nearly an outgrowth of his friendships, and his special companions inspired his verses, either from afar or while attending the poet at his work.

From about 1261 to 1273 Rumi and Hosam al-Din spent countless hours together working on this vast opus, an undertaking so large that Rumi once observed puckishly that, when completed, the book would need forty camels to carry it. During their marathon sessions, Rumi would compose aloud, while Hosam would scurry to put the poet's musings down on paper; then Hosam in his dedicated manner would sing back to Rumi what he had written for the poet's approval. According to Sepahsalar, during these sessions Hosam al-Din was sometimes so transported by Rumi's mystic revelations that he would pass out. We are told that when he regained consciousness he would cry in ecstasy and bow down in front of Rumi in gratitude.

Hosam's central role in the composition of the *Mathnawi* can be evidenced through an anecdote from Aflaki. Supposedly, Hosam al-Din was overtaken by grief when his wife unexpectedly passed away. For weeks he was unable to focus or work on the *Mathnawi*. During this time Rumi also showed no inclination to take up the project again. Yet, when Hosam had recovered and pronounced himself ready to work again, Rumi also renewed his interest in the project.

The introduction of the *Mathnawi* makes clear just how crucial Hosam al-Din was in the endeavor; Rumi provides a lengthy description of the Friend's attributes that is nearly as long, windy and baffling as the masterwork itself:

I have exerted myself to give length to the poem in rhyr couplets, which comprises strange tales and rare sayinp excellent discourses and precious indications . . . at the request of my master and stay and support [who holds] the place of the spirit in my body, and (who is) the treasure of my today and my tomorrow, namely, the Sheikh. . . .[12]

In a sense the tale of Rumi's own life can be told most clearly through studying his relationships to his three special companions. The protean Rumi seems often to have summoned special qualities out of the psyches of these three men, drawing on these needed traits to lead his life, and produce his work. Rumi believed that his rare associations with his special companions produced an affinity that led to a more profound fusion with his God. At the same time these friendships seemed to be the core and sustenance of his mundane life.

While enthralled with Shams, Rumi learned the power and profundity of mysticism, and to look beyond the limitations of intellectual understanding. From Shams he also learned how to suspend the conventions of society, when necessary. Salah al-Din was to soothe the disoriented Rumi after his violent metamorphosis during his years with Shams. The humble love and unquestioning friendship of Salah al-Din also helped give Rumi sufficient peace of mind to begin composing ghazals. Hosam al-Din was the patient scribe who worked alongside Rumi for countless hours producing the *Mathnawi*; a profound mystic himself, he also functioned as Rumi's muse in these sessions, providing inspiration for these mysterious verses.

Each of Rumi's special companions played a crucial role, and the exchanges and intertwining of identities were very complex. It is even possible to conjecture that without the three Beloveds, the poetry cherished by so many people could never have been written. Rumi shared far more with these companions than he did with his family and students, who sometimes seem to have been mere distractions from the poet's true pursuits. The three men seem almost to have been appendages of Rumi, and vice versa.

Once asked to explain the various roles played by his three Beloved friends, the poet, according to Sultan Valad, likened Shams to the sun, the gentle, reflective Salah al-Din to the moon, and Hosam al-Din to the stars "for having joined the angels."

Exterior. Mevlana Mausoleum, Konya, Turkey.
(Vanni/Art Resource, NY)

10

The Most Digressive Story Ever Told

> It is mere legends and paltry tales; there is no
> profound inquiry and lofty speculation.
> The little children understand it; 'tis naught
> but things approved and disapproved.[1]
>
> —*Jalalu'ddin Rumi*

WELL BEFORE IT EVER WAS COMPLETED, the *Mathnawi* had begun to generate bewilderment and annoyance among some of its readers, a state of affairs which has persisted until today. Readers quickly began to ask exactly what sort of a masterpiece was this "low," superficially simple work consisting of "imitation" that even "the little children understand?" Did it have anything to do with Islam? If so, why didn't it contain "profound inquiry and lofty speculation?" And what on earth, or in heaven, was its elusive subject?

It took more than a decade for Rumi to compose the about 25,700 verses of the *Mathnawi*, a late-life masterwork that evidently defied the expectations of some of his contemporaries. Such readers apparently had anticipated a sort of textbook, setting forth the ways and means of Islamic mysticism with mechanical precision. They do not seem to have braced themselves for this cheerful and very long string of earthy stories, jokes, and profound but unpretentious philosophic meanderings.

Once more, some members of Konya's ulema were moved to criticize Rumi's populist tastes and accessible literary techniques for diverging from their own conventions. And again, one could ask—given that Rumi had resided in Konya for over three decades by this time—why these scholars and citizens still had not grasped his long-established and anti-elititist preference for language and forms understood by all segments of society.

In the above lines from the third book of his opus, Rumi takes time out from his digressive storytelling and philosophizing to address the work's detractors. He addresses those critics who allege that the *Mathnawi* "is low; [that] it is the story of the Prophet and [consists of] imitation [of the Koran]." He also answers those who faulted his volumes for their apparent lack of philosophic inquiry and failure to provide a diagram-like description of the means by which mystics achieve union with the Absolute.

Rumi defends his work as being well within the received traditions of Islam. Indeed, he views the *Mathnawi* chiefly as a companion piece to the Koran. He notes that the Koran also was sharply criticized at first for being a somewhat sad collection of "mere legends and paltry tales"; this was a deft rejoinder to critics who found fault with such techniques in Rumi's work, without noticing that this type of storytelling also appears throughout the Koran—a religious work revered in the Islamic world as the literal speech of God, dictated to Mohammad without human editing. Driving home his point that the criticisms of his work could just as easily be leveled against the Koran, Rumi observes that it is possible "on the part of them that have lost the [right] way" to complain that the Koran itself is "naught but words." Rumi then goes on to rebuke his critics with the observation that producing allegories and poems which are easily understood, pleasing and spiritually enlightening, is in fact a nearly impossible task: "Let the Jinn and mankind and the skilled among you produce a single verse of this 'easy style.'"[2]

IN TIME, RUMI'S defense of his work was to become broadly accepted; indeed, the *Mathnawi* has come to be known popularly as "the Persian Koran." And, like the Koran, it is peppered throughout with references to the Judeo-Christian Bible. There are frequent parables; many lifted directly from the Bible, involving Moses, Jesus and the Virgin Mary, all of whom are viewed as important religious figures who prepared mankind for its ultimate Prophet, Mohammad. The *Mathnawi*, also frequently invokes the name of Mohammad, who is viewed as God's messenger, not God Himself. And God Himself is a constant presence of the *Mathnawi*, much as he was in the writings of Rumi's father, the much-afflicted Baha al-Din, who frequently addressed the Absolute in his *Ma'aref*, as if He were Baha al-Din's sole friend and comforter. Rumi, in many passages of the *Mathnawi*, addresses his God directly and with equal degrees of ease and familiarity.

But despite the work's blatant religious content and purpose, some of Rumi's contemporaries were troubled by it. Franklin Lewis deduces that these readers probably had trouble reconciling the genial and eccentric observations of the *Mathnawi* with more customary forms of Islamic religious discourse:

> The *Mathnawi* is a kind of Koran commentary, but not in the conventional verse-by-verse manner; it concentrates on the spiritual message of the scripture, as reflected through the discourses of theology, law and Sufism. It describes a path for the purification and sanctification of the soul that leads the soul back to its heavenly abode.[3]

Another reason that it may have been difficult for Rumi's contemporaries to grasp his work and its intentions is that he was working in a relatively new genre for the Persian language. In the twelfth century Sana'i, Rumi's poetic predecessor, invented a form of Persian religious explanatory poetry, composed to be read aloud to groups of religious scholars, preachers and lawyer-divines. Previously, Persian poetry had been produced chiefly for the benefit of sultans and high-ranking soldiers, and it often was devised to flatter powerful patrons at court. After Sana'i, it became more common for Persian poets to find their inspiration in spiritual truths, rather than politicking. But during Rumi's lifetime, this type of religious and poetic expression was still rather new and may have been puzzling to some. Criticisms of the *Mathnawi* were to continue throughout its creation. In Book VI, the final volume, Rumi quips: "Does a caravan ever turn back from a journey on account of the noise and clamor of the dogs?"

IT'S IMPORTANT TO UNDERSTAND that the *Mathnawi*, was and is baffling not just to its critics. Those who love it also have much trouble defining its nature, value and structure, including even its great British translator Reynold A. Nicholson, who rendered all six of its exasperatingly complex and detouring volumes into a comprehensive and complete English translation. In an introduction to his translation of Books I and II, written in 1925, he reveals that he regards the book's significance to be that it reflects "[however darkly at times] so much of the highest as well as the lowest in the life and thought of the Mohammadan world in the later Middle Ages."

Nicholson begins this introduction by placing the *Mathnawi*, firmly within the confines of the world's great masterpieces, noting that it contains about as many syllables as the *Iliad*, and *Odyssey*, combined, and also is about twice the length of the *Divine Comedy*. But then he quickly goes on to reveal his own questions about its value by quoting the somewhat acerbic observation of his fellow translator, the German Georg Rosen: "Who would care to devote a considerable part of his lifetime to translating thirty thousand or forty thousand Persian distichs of unequal poetical worth?"[4] Nicholson also laments that—given the complexities of Persian verse and the immense differences between medieval Islamic culture and the modern world—any faithful modern English translation would have to be at least somewhat unintelligible to today's readers. On the other hand, an easily understood translation of the *Mathnawi* would have to take many liberties with language and meaning and might well undermine Rumi's intentions.

And these are not the only frustrations connected with this work! We also must worry about the ephemeral nature of Rumi's thinking processes, his peculiar ventriloquist's talent for leaping suddenly between narrative voices and styles, and the work's utter lack of predictable sequencing. Nicholson notes that inevitably a book that records the sessions of a great master with his disciples will lose something in the translation, given that some profound utterances will be almost indecipherable to anyone outside the master's immediate circle. In addition, "The loose and rambling structure of the poem leads to other perplexities. When our author gives no sign whether he is speaking in his own person or by the voice of one of his innumerable puppets—celestial, infernal, human, or animal—who talk just like himself; when he mingles his comments into the exposition; when he leaves us in doubt as to whom he is addressing or what he is describing . . ."[5]

Reynold A. Nicholson's painstaking translation has made it possible for readers throughout the English-speaking world to enjoy Rumi's poetry. However, it currently is not the best-selling English language version of his work. That distinction goes to a group of contemporary American poets, including Coleman Barks and Robert Bly, who seem to concentrate more on creating fresh interpretations of relatively small sections of Rumi's poetry, including the ghazals, rather than translating the lengthy volumes of the *Mathnawi* in their entirety.

In his book *The Life and Work of Jalaluddin Rumi*, Afzal Iqbal, while conceding that the field of Islamic studies owes a great debt to Nicholson, also worries that the Victorian translator inadvertently helped circulate misconceptions about the *Mathnawi*. In his introduction, Nicholson discusses his decision to render a few seemingly ribald passages of the *Mathnawi* into Latin, rather than English. The use of Latin in such cases was once a fairly common method of making questionable excerpts more accessible to Western readers, while still signaling the translator's disapproval of them. In Nicholson's view, a literal English translation of some of these passages would place Rumi in danger of being compared to the lascivious Roman satirist Petronius; the use of Latin apparently somehow prevents this sort of association. Iqbal asserts that Nicholson was unduly worried about the use of material that could be perceived as obscene, given that these passages were nearly always followed with strict sermonizing. No aspect of life was off limits to the worldly Rumi, who frequently displayed a sly Sufi humor. At the same time, the earthier anecdotes of the *Mathnawi* were never offered merely for their own sake.

In the fourth book, Nicholson resorts to Latin in part to explain that the wife of a Sufi sometimes entertains a lover during the day while her husband is at work. We then return to English to learn that her husband had become suspicious of the pair and one day, when they were inside his small house, knocked on the door with all his might. The deceitful couple decided upon a ruse, covering the man in a chador. Finally, the wife lets her husband inside the house and explains that she is being visited by a great lady of the town. This lady, supposedly, has learned of the virtue of the Sufi and his wife, and has decided to marry her son to their daughter. Aware of the deception, the Sufi protests that they are far too poor and humble to wed their daughter to such a well-to-do young man. His wife insists, however, that the lady does not care about wealth.

From one viewpoint, the scene could be made to be very amusing in a Chaucerian way; but Rumi does not develop it frivolously for its full comic potential. For instance, the Sufi does not tear the chador away from the head of his rival, and the lover does not run screeching from the house. Nor does a brawl between the two men ensue, and the Sufi does not rail and expose his wife's droll untruths in any direct manner; we also are not treated to a further display of her desperate and childish manipulations. As is often the case with Rumi, the subject and tone of the work simply shift and we instead are offered some philosophic observations. We learn:

> I have told this story with the intent that thou mayst not
> weave idle talk when the offense is glaring.
> Thou hast been unfaithful, like the Sufi's wife; thou hast
> opened in fraud the snare of cunning . . .
> Thou art ashamed before every dirty braggart, and not
> before thy God.[6]

By the time a reader finishes reading these lines, he has been forcefully reminded that lies and hypocrisies are exposed in time. Many tales in the *Mathnawi*, including this one, culminate in easily understood morals like those found in *Aesop's Fables*. The *Mathnawi* draws material and techniques from some sources outside the Koran, including Anatolian folk stories that bear a strong resemblance to *Aesop's Fables*, popular medieval tales about the Sufis, and anecdotes clearly lifted from the works of Attar and Sana'i. All these stories are told in such an amusing and digressive way that their points are made gently and through implication.

In addition to being a commentary on the Koran, the *Mathnawi* is also an entertaining set of books. After all, this work, by legend at least, was Rumi's response to Hosam al-Din's request that the poet compose a broad and ranging masterpiece, one that would captivate the troubadours and inspire them to compose music to its rhymes. However, not only a collection of accessible and enjoyable tales and morals, the *Mathnawi* is at the same time a deliberately difficult book. A great deal of its subject matter is beyond rational understanding and the reader is forced to absorb many of these poems intuitively and subliminally. As Annemarie Schimmel states: "The whole *Mathnawi* is an attempt to show the way that leads towards the inner meaning which is 'hidden like the lion in the forest,' dangerous and overwhelming. . . . Even if the trees were pens and the oceans ink, the *Mathnawi* could not be completed—it is infinite since it tries to expound the infiniteness of God."[7]

AND WHAT IS ONE to make of the manner in which many stories in the *Mathnawi* slip almost imperceptibly into other anecdotes, forcing the reader to stay ever alert to the topic at hand? In the many spots where abrupt transitions take place, the reader can only imagine what caused the shift in focus. Perhaps Hosam al-Din was growing tired and had put his pen away for the day; then when he was ready to work again, he found himself or Rumi in a completely different frame of mind. Or perhaps Hosam al-Din, or some other disciple, broke into Rumi's train of thought, by bringing up some other subject, obliging the ever-courteous poet to shift his mental gears.

On the other hand, it sometimes may have been that Rumi developed some of these anecdotes more fully, and Hosam al-Din was not able to record all of them word for word, and detail for detail. Then again, there is the very real possibility that Rumi, in his own way, actually had finished his topics. A teacher, as well as a poet, Rumi—in some cases—may have developed topics as far as they needed to be for his instructional purposes, rather than carrying them through to their dramatic and poetical conclusions.

At any rate, the established staples of Western literature— the fully-developed characters, the cleverly plotted narrative and the flawless and satisfying denouement— don't always matter to

Rumi. But then, again, sometimes they do! The *Mathnawi* is too full of inconsistency even to be consistent in its inconsistency.

At the same time, sometimes we do return to a seemingly abandoned topic or character. For instance, the admonition to "not weave idle talk when the offense is glaring," at the end of the tale of the Sufi's unfaithful wife is in fact spoken by a woman character who disappeared from the text three pages earlier. She tells the story to rebuke a man, telling him his lascivious behavior is analogous to that of the unfaithful wife. The very unpredictability of the *Mathnawi* enlivens the experience of reading it by keeping the reader in a permanent state of suspense. The reader is forced to remain ever alert to the narrative because he has no way to predict where it is leading, or when the narrator will abruptly shift identities.

Although the *Mathnawi* has inspired more than its fair share of controversy and skepticism over the centuries, it also has been treasured by many. It is pleasant to learn that Rumi himself was thoroughly confident of its enduring beauty and profundity. He, like many readers, considered Book IV, with its numerous discussions of various states of spiritual illumination, and the nature of consciousness and the universe, to represent the epitome of the entire undertaking.

In the introduction to his favorite volume, Rumi confidently writes:

The fourth journey to the best of abodes and the greatest of advantages. . . . There is cheer for spirits and healing for bodies; and it is like what the sincere [in devotion to God] crave and love, and what the travelers [on the Way to God] seek and wish for—a refreshment to eyes and a joy to souls, the sweetest of fruits to them that cull, and the most sublime of things desired and coveted; bringing the sick man to his physician and guiding the lover to his beloved.[8]

Exterior. Tomb of Rumi.
(SEF/Art Resource, NY)

11

Death Dervish-Style

Leaving manhood behind, there's no doubt you'll become an angel;
The earth you'll leave then, and head for Heaven.
Transcending the angel, become an ocean, whose each drop
will be larger than the countless Seas of Oman.[1]

—Jalalu'ddin Rumi

IN LATE 1273 RUMI WAS sixty-six years old and, by some suggestions, perfectly ready and willing to die, contrasting with his
own father who was nearly sixty when the poet was born and
who lived to be nearly eighty-five years old. Throughout his
poetry, Rumi seems at peace with the human body's inherent
cycle of aging, as well as the prospect of transcendent experiences after death, or as he puts it, the process of "transcending
the angel," to "become an ocean."

With Rumi there also is a sense that he couldn't have gone on
too much longer: the exhausting events of his singular life had
exacted quite a toll. The creation of the *Mathnawi*, a momentous
and fatiguing project undertaken when the poet was well into
middle age, possibly hastened Rumi's willingness to make his
departure. At any rate, Rumi seems to have lost some of his verve
as the elongated masterwork heaved to its conclusion. As
Annemarie Schimmel points out, the final story of the sixth and
final book of the *Mathnawi* even lacks a definitive conclusion.
Toward the very end of Book VI, Rumi serves up a psychologi-
cally delicious story about a deceased man who had bequeathed

that his estate be passed to the laziest of his three sons. The man's sons all proclaim that they will stand by the terms of their father's will. "We are like Ishmael: We will not recoil from our Abraham, although he is offering us in sacrifice," they say.

The reader of the will, or cadi, then asks each of the heirs to give an account of his own particular type of laziness. He also makes a few provocative distinctions about various types of people and various forms of laziness. For instance, he chides the Gnostics "because they get their harvest without ploughing." This late life stinging criticism of the gnostics from Rumi, one of history's greatest gnostics, is quite intriguing. However, the remark also is somewhat sketchy, and, unfortunately, the topic is abruptly scuttled.

The cadi goes on to describe other extremes of laziness, leaving one to wait for the ridiculous but delectable little scene in which each of the brothers must attempt to outdo his siblings as a champion of sloth. But that scene also never arrives. The narrator evidently is growing tired, and chooses to wind the story down before it is fully developed. This section concludes with a philosophic discussion of how one can "distinguish a [sincere] friend from a double-hearted person," and two of the brothers tell how they make such distinctions. But we never learn which brother is laziest, and the will's contents are never distributed.

After this abbreviated tale, we are presented with a short and ambiguous parable, which provides the conclusion for the entire *Mathnawi*. This final passage also displays Rumi's mischievous sense of humor, and continues the discussion of how one can recognize sincerity, or its lack of, in another. A kindly mother tells her child how to repel a ghost, should such a disembodied spirit frighten her child in a graveyard at night:

"Keep a stout heart, and rush at it, and immediately it will turn its face away from you."

"[But]," says the woman's child, "suppose the devilish bogle's mother has said this [same thing] to it; [If] I rush at it, but its mother's orders it will fall on my neck: what shall I do then?" "You are teaching me to stand firm, [but] the ugly bogle has a mother, too."[2]

Again we are set up to await a plot development—in this case a sound maternal comeback to a child's unexpectedly clever argument. But, again, we have a hasty derailment of our expectations. Instead, we are given this metaphysical meditation, also to some extent ambiguous, on the questions of how it could be that both good children and hideous ghosts could have caring mothers, and how it is that both fine men and fiendish devils share a single creator: "The instructor of [the race of] devils and of mankind is the One [God]: through Him the enemy prevails [even] if he is in small force. On whichever side that Gracious One may be, go and for God' sake, for God's sake, be on that side!"[3]

Finally, the reader of the will, or cadi, observes that a worthy man is unlikely to be deceived by tricks while considering another person's sincerity. In conclusion, Rumi leaves us with a subtle discussion, in which he concludes that it is the heart that enables one person to know another. When the question is posed by the cadi how the worthy man can know the other's hidden nature, he replies, "I sit before him in silence. The speech in my heart comes from that auspicious quarter, for there is a window between heart and heart."[4]

AND, SO THE LONGEST, most elusive and perhaps greatest work of medieval literature ends with Rumi making a final exploration of the mysteries of the human heart. Yet we learn little specific information from the final lines of the *Mathnawi* about the condition of Rumi's own heart as his death approached. Nor is the intriguing topic of legal and spiritual legacies and wills developed in such a way that gives us clues about his deathbed feelings about his own disciples and children—who were quite capable of treachery and "double-hearted" behavior on occassion—or his ideas about how he and his work would be perceived after his passing. But at least we learn that death and legacies were, quite naturally, to some extent occupying his mind.

Rumi's life was not to last much longer. According to Annemarie Schimmel, Rumi was to continue dictating the *Mathnawi* to the faithful Hosam al-Din up until just shortly before his fatal illness. By legend, he continued composing scattered ghazals on his sickbed, in order to comfort a large number of concerned guests.

In addition to the exhausting nature of his endeavors, there were other wearying developments in the weeks and months leading up to the poet's death. The political situation in Anatolia, through which Rumi had always navigated successfully, was worsening. The Seljuks remained nominal rulers and often managed to establish and advance the cultural and religious institutions which were so precious to them, and which gave Anatolia its enlightened flavor. Yet for decades the Seljuks had merely provided a façade for the Mongols, while exercising limited political power themselves. To keep from being toppled, the Seljuks had to pay constant tributes to their vassals, whose control over the area was tightening, and whose tactics were increasingly barbarous.

During these months, Rumi heard disturbing reports of Mongol soldiers breaking into private homes for no reason and stories of bizarre, unprovoked attacks on scholars. Despite his excellent relationships with the ruling class, he may have had worries for the safety of his household and of his friends. By 1274, the year after Rumi's death, a number of these scholars and other Konya residents were to leave the beautiful city for the relative safety of the Mamluk Kingdom in Syria and Egypt. By dying when he did, in late 1273, Rumi missed seeing the downfall of Mu'in al-Din, who had been the Mongol vasal of Anatolia for twenty years and a close friend of Rumi's. Mu'in al-Din was replaced by a party of Turk noblemen, who were in league with the Egyptian Baibars. They planned to otherthrow the Mongols, then join forces with the Mamluk princes; however, this plot failed.

But in discussing Rumi's unusual readiness for his own demise, it's important to note that he was not merely exhausted by his endeavors, and worried about the future. There also is a sense that the ever-curious Rumi was ready, and possibly even eager, to experience death, a subject he touched on often in his poetry. For a person of Rumi's great wisdom and fearlessness, death was a new frontier, and possibly even an adventure. It seems the poet was awaiting a great experience of transcendence.

Sepahsalar often noted the joyous and welcoming attitude toward death reflected in Rumi's poems, and expressed doubt that any other writer could ever exceed his poetic grasp of this subject. Indeed, Rumi, in his poems, often likened the moment of death to a wedding, inasmuch as it represented a new union—in this case an intermingling of his own life with that of his God. Sepahsalar believed that Rumi had no cause to fear death because he had led an exemplary life. In Sepahsalar's cosmology, a soul that has acquired spiritual honors during its life on earth instantly will become a reflection of the divine at the moment of death. The hagiographer believed that in Rumi's case, death would mean fusion with the Absolute and release of his soul from the prison of self.

Afzal Iqbal suggests that Rumi didn't fear death because he was a great artist. He states that, "for as a creative artist he draws his inspiration from his own immortal self for which there is neither decay nor death but which on the other hand, grows and develops continuously."[5] The third book of the *Mathnawi* contains a somewhat acerbic reflection on how some human beings avoid thinking about death. Rumi tells us that many people regard death as something that will never happen to them, as a problem for others, but not themselves. To avoid the inevitable fact of death, such people deceive themselves that the possessions they own, and the talents they display will endure forever. Rumi notes that supposedly learned scholars also sometimes immerse themselves in mundane concerns to avoid reflection on the unavoidable reality of death:

> Bare he came and naked he goes, and [all the while] his heart is bleeding with anxiety on account of the thief.
> At the hour of death when a hundred lamentations are [being made] beside him, his spirit begins to laugh at its own fear.
> At that moment the rich man knows that he has no gold; the keen-witted man, too, knows that he is devoid of talent.[6]

Rumi's own relaxed attitude towards death contrasted sharply with that of the people he criticized in the above verses. Having thought often about death, he did not deceive himself about life's short duration and he, unlike his devoted disciples, was not worried about his own approaching demise. According to Aflaki, he was visited during the final stage of his fatal illness by a friend who wished him a quick and full recovery. Rumi is said to have replied: "When between the lover and the Beloved there is only a poor shirt left, wouldn't you want the light to unite with the Light?"

SEPAHSALAR CLAIMS THAT Konya had been rocked with earthquakes for forty days before Rumi's death. Many people came to Rumi to ask him to pray and ward off a catastrophe. By legend, Rumi replied that they had no need to worry. The earth was hungering for a juicy morsel in the form of his corpse, but it would be satisfied soon and no harm would come to the town. However, according to the hagiographers' accounts, the number and intensity of these earthquakes increased the nervousness that many other people felt about the poet's impending death. In time, the hagiographers' recollections of the earthquakes preceding Rumi's death would embellish his legend, creating a sense of great foreboding, as if the earth itself was trembling in shock because it somehow understood it was about to be deprived of one of its greatest treasures.

The hagiographers tell us that Rumi was attended by two great doctors, including his close friend, a physician named Akmalodding Tabib. The doctors were puzzled by his illness and could find nothing other than an excess of water and a general frailty. At length, they concluded that Rumi wished to die, according to the legend. During his time of illness, Rumi was surrounded by a stream of disciples and other visitors. He evidently recited to them poems touching on the theme of death as a door to a new life. He also encouraged them to celebrate his death joyfully with sama and to view it as a beautiful act of transcendence. Perhaps he read these defiantly joyful verses from the *Divan-e* to discourage his visitors from feeling mournful:

> When you come visiting my grave, my roofed tomb will
> appear to you in dancing. . . .
> Do not come without tambourine to my tomb, brother!
> For a grieved person does no fit in Gods' banquet!

According to the translator W. M. Thackston, Rumi, during his final illness told his many friends: "In this world I have had two attachments, one to the body and one to you. When, of God's grace, I shall be disemboweled in the world of solitude and abstraction, my attachment to you will still exist."

Sufism a Threat to Leaders

Throughout its history, Sufism has often had a very charged relationship with political authority in part because some writers, including Attar, wrote very critically about such leaders. In addition, the elusive nature of the teachings, the strong emphasis on personal truth and liberty, as well as powerful fraternal bonds, have made Sufism a threat to leaders at many points. Medieval rulers of Islamic states were highly aware that the master-disciple relationship, a pivotal aspect of Sufism, sometimes was much more powerful than the loyalty that a subject had for his king or political sheikh. During the colonial era, when many European powers sought to annex Islamic states, Sufi orders proved to be a surprisingly strong network of resistance in lands as diverse as Libya, the Caucasus and the Sudan.

In order to find ways to understand and subdue the Sufis and other potentially rebellious elements, colonial administrators often commissioned detailed social studies of their activities. Much of the knowledge about Islamic societies accumulated by European scholars during the colonial period was amassed to enable colonial administrators to control local populations. In one ironic study, the French government in 1900 concluded that the conquest of Algeria had strengthened the Rahmaniyya Sufi Order there. British colonialists were keenly aware of the social influence of the Sufi orders in India, and sometimes attempted to use that force for their own ends by appointing Sufis to posts of governmental authority.

The Mevlevi Order came under the control of the Ottoman Empire in the seventeenth century. Although the order lost much of its independence when it came under Ottoman domination, royal patronage allowed the Mevlevis to spread to many lands and to introduce many people to the order's unique musical and poetic traditions. In the eighteenth century, Selim III, an Ottoman sultan, became a member of the order. He later composed music for Mevlevi ceremonies.

During the nineteenth century, the Mevlevis were one of around nineteen Sufi orders in

Turkey and about thirty-five such orders in the Ottoman Empire. Due to their royal patrons, the Mevlevis were one of the most influential orders in the entire empire and their cultural achievements were considered highly refined. The order also became well known in the West where their whirling performances had seized the public imagination. During the nineteenth century, a lodge maintained by the order in Istanbul attracted large groups of European tourists to its weekly *sama* performances.

The Mevlevis were forced to disband in their Turkish homeland abruptly in 1925, after Kemal Ataturk, the founder of the modern state, banned all dervish orders and their rituals and performances. At that time, Rumi's shrine in Konya was taken over by the government, which converted it into a state museum. Ataturk's chief motivation was to sever Turkey from its medieval past in order to thrust it into the modern world as a Western-style democracy. For Ataturk, Sufism was threatening not because of its stress on inner freedom, but because of its unearthly mysticism and traditions.

To this day, Rumi's tomb in Konya is maintained and run by the Turkish government as a tourist attraction, although many of its visitors come as religious pilgrims, rather than gawking tourists. In a compromise, the Turkish government in 1953 agreed to allow Mevlevi dances to be performed in Konya, but only with the understanding that these performances are cultural events for the benefit of tourists. Dervish troupes are allowed to travel internationally also. Yet many aspects of Sufism remain illegal in Turkey, and Sufis have been subjected to persecution ever since Ataturk outlawed their religion.

AS RUMI'S DEATH APPROACHED, the issue of who should be his successor arose once more, and again there were disciples who pushed for the selection of Sultan Valad. Aflaki states that some of the eminent disciples of Rumi gathered around his deathbed to inquire about his choice of successor. Three times the question was asked, and three times the answer was, "Hosam al-Din." When asked about Sultan Valad, Rumi, again passed on a chance to appoint his favorite son, replying, "He is a hero and has not need for my will." Sepahsalar records that Rumi composed a poem on his deathbed to encourage Sultan Valad to go and get some sleep and not worry about his father's passing. If this story is true, the poem appears not to have ever been preserved.

Rumi passed away on December 17, 1273 at sunset, according to the hagiographers. They also tell us that Konya then fell utterly silent. By legend, Rumi's cat, wishing to join him, refused food and died one week after him, His daughter buried the cat close to her father, who often celebrated animals in his work. To this day, December 17 is famous throughout Turkey as "the wedding night," a reference to Rumi's frequent observations that his death would be like a marriage celebration that would consecrate his union with the Absolute.

After Rumi passed away, the entire town of Konya fell into an intense state of mourning. Despite Rumi's pleas that his passing be celebrated with tambourine music and displays of mirth, Konya took its loss very hard. By all accounts, Rumi was missed deeply and equally by persons of all backgrounds—rich and poor alike—and religious persuasions. Christians and Jews joined the Muslims in these rituals, wailing and tearing away at their collars and heaping dust on their heads. All of Konya united in a civic rite that lasted a full forty days and included performances by mastersingers of odes Rumi had written in gleeful anticipation of the occasion. Says Aflaki, "There was an uproar so loud that it could have been the day of the great Resurrection."

Members of all Anatolian religious communities were full participants in this ritual, and holy men from each group held up high copies of the Koran, the Bible and other key spiritual texts. Aflaki recalls that the non-Muslims explained their devotion by saying, "When we saw him, we understood the real nature of Christ, of Moses and of all the Prophets." By legend, the wailing did not end even after the mourners returned to their houses. Shortly after Rumi's death Sultan Valad was to memorialize his father saying, "Folks from every faith proved faithful to him—in love with him the people of all nations."[7]

Despite Rumi's instructions that Hosam al-Din be installed as his successor, some disciples and relatives gathered at Rumi's grave and again took up the issue of whether Sultan Valad should be named to this post. There also was talk of Hosam al-Din and Sultan Valad sharing the leadership of the disciples and the order that, over time, would become the Mevlevi Order. At this time, Hosam al-Din said he was willing to step down and would defer to Sultan Valad. But Salad Valad would not accept the post, well aware that doing so would violate his father's deathbed wishes.

When Salah al-Din died, Sultan Valad had been thirty-two years, and a ripe age for leadership. Franklin Lewis suggests that at that time Sultan Valad may have expected to be appointed, and there are indications that he was disappointed by Rumi's selection of Hosam al-Din. However, by the time that Rumi died, his son had come to accept the choice of Hosam al-Din. But in quite an interesting denouement, Hosam al-Din was to pass away about five years after Rumi's death, when Sultan Valad was forty-seven years old. Once more, some of the disciples demanded that Sultan Valad be the successor. But this time Sultan Valad himself appeared to sincerely not want the post that eluded him so many times in the past; so he refused it. However, the disciples were quite determined and coaxed him to accept the position; eventually he did so.

THE MEVLEVI ORDER was institutionalized by Sultan Valad sometime after the death of Hosam al-Din. The order avoided fanaticism and welcomed members of all religions, in keeping with Rumi's tolerant spirit. The order also maintained the same strictness about fasting and purification that Rumi had advocated throughout his life. All dervishes ate from the same plate and did so while reclining slightly, in order to discourage overeating.

Many members of the Mevlevi Order came from artisan and merchant backgrounds and all worked for their livings. In keeping with his father's wishes, Sultan Valad did not allow the dervishes to burden society. Instead, they were directed to contribute to it. Some other dervishes begged for their livings, but members of the Mevlevi Order could not beg for alms unless they had gone three days without food. The order was highly disciplined in other ways, too. Although the customary period of retreat in an Islamic brotherhood was forty days, Mevlevi dervish initiates had to remain at the monastery for 1,001 days. Initiates were kept busy all day, performing tedious and humbling tasks, such as sweeping floors and cleaning baths. They were not allowed to rest or eat until after evening prayers.

The order flourished in the decentralized, tolerant manner set down by Sultan Valad for about two hundred years after his father's death. The Konya monastery, or *takya*, was followed by other *takyas* elsewhere in Anatolia. The order often went to small villages to live among the unpretentious people who had been precious to Rumi, sharing sama, music and poetry with them; quite surprisingly, women often were allowed to join in these rituals. The *Mathnawi* was translated into Turkish and other vernacular languages, so that people would not have to learn Persian to appreciate it.

However, the tolerant, humanistic, decentralized nature of the order changed in the fifteenth century when Ottoman sultans perceived that they could manipulate it as a kind of defense against political insurgents. The order was centralized and began to depend on financial contributions. During the Ottoman Empire, the Mevlevi *takyas* spread from Azerbaijan to Vienna, but much of their original character had been forfeited to political expediency as the order became an aristocratic institution. Still, the Mevlevi Order had a tremendous influence on music, art, calligraphy and poetry throughout the empire. Many of the *takyas* declined or closed as the empire itself decayed. Later the order would shrink further in 1925 when Ataturk, the first leader of modern Turkey, took measures against what he perceived to be an antiquated institution. However, there are today some Mevlevi *takyas* in Turkey, as well as in Cyprus, Egypt and Libya.

A few years after his death, a lavish tomb was built to cover Rumi's grave. The tomb, a gift from some of his wealthy admirers, was decorated in rich tones of gold and black and deliberately arranged to resemble a bridal suite, reflecting the poet's likening of his death to a spiritual wedding. Inside the tomb, Rumi's dervish hat hangs. On top of his gold coffin, some of his most beautiful verses are inscribed and there are Arabic words praising his greatness. A thick and beautiful gold blanket covers the tomb. Above Rumi's tomb there is an inscription from the Koran, and this tribute:

. . . here is the resting place of Rumi, Sultan of the Wise, shining light of God illuminating the darkness, an iman son of an iman, support of Islam, a guide to the people who leads them into God's glorious presence.

His admirers also built a magnificent structure over his tomb, the Green Dome, which in time became the center of a complex for the Mevlevi Order. This complex contains a monastery with cells, a large kitchen and a library. The ornate beauty of Rumi's resting place has made it an enduring tourist attraction. Nearly every day brings new visits from poetry lovers and religious pilgrims. By tradition, all visitors to the order are greeted graciously. The tomb and the Mevlevi complex comprise a site where his admirers can make a connection to the long-dead poet; some later remark that they were able to sense his spirit there.

Despite the beauty of this monument and the comfort it provides to pilgrims, there is a problem with the tomb site: it was not the sort of resting place the poet desired, or imagined for himself. Rumi apparently left instructions to his disciples to not construct an elaborate tomb or other edifice to his memory. Instead, he had wanted, in the manner of many nature-loving dervishes, to have a simple grave over which the sun and rain and dust could pass. However—in much the same manner that his request for a mirthful funeral was passed over—his request for a discrete grave was disregarded also. There is a sense that because Rumi belonged to Konya, the town believed it could do whatever it wanted with him. By encasing him in a massive and conventional tomb, the citizens of Konya finally obtained a small degree of domination over this most uncontrollable of poets. It seems that, even in death, Rumi's adoring public could not bear to leave him alone.

ACKNOWLEDGEMENTS

I received invaluable help from many sources on this fascinating project, especially from my editor, Barbara Leah Ellis, who suggested this book to me. Anwarul Chodhury and Mohsen Ashtiani provided excellent suggestions for research sources. In addition, the staff, bookshelves and convivial atmosphere of Manhattan's Sufi Books also provided inspiration.

A number of other people also provided practical support, sound advice and honest readers' responses, including Susan Mastondrea, Charles Ragland, Riva Lavva, and Zarina Ahmad, Barbara Lewis, Coretha Fulton, Amir Bahati, Louise Fleming, Sabina Ostowlski, Nick Godt and Donald Giampietro.

I also was encouraged at many points by the large number of other writers, scholars, and artists of various types, pursuing other projects which concern Rumi and his writings.

CHRONOLOGY

Note to readers: Nearly all dates related to Rumi's life are approximations, given discrepancies in varied accounts and differences between the lunar and solar calendars.

1152	Birth of Baha al-Din, father of Rumi, in province of Khorosan in what is now Afghanistan; probably in or near city of Balkh
1204–1210	Baha al-Din and family settle in Khorosan city of Vakhsh where he performs a variety of preaching and teaching duties
1207	Sept. 30: Commonly accepted birth date of Jalal al-Din Rumi to Baha al-Din and Mo'mene Khatun, one of his four wives. An older brother, Ala al-Din, had been born to the couple some years earlier.
1208–1210	Baha al-Din encounters opposition and ridicule in Vakhsh; chief judge of city questions his right to use title "Chief of the Jurisconsultants"

874	Bistami, a controversial Sufi who angered many by declaring himself to be God, dies in Neishapour; founded Sufi ecstatic, as opposed to sober, school
922	Sufi "heretic" Mansur al-Hallaj executed for revelation of Sufi doctrines previously kept secret
1058	Iranian mystic Abu Hamid Mohammad al-Ghazzali is born in the city of Tus. His *Alchemy of Happiness*, a severe critique of Greek philosophy, was to exert a deep influence on Baha al-Din and Rumi.
1092	Frank crusaders launch first attempt by Christian world to conquer the Islamic lands, toppling nearly all Islamic leaders from Egypt eastward, severely weakening Seljuk dynasty, among others
1120	Farid ud-Din Attar, Sufi poet who allegedly met Rumi when poet was a young boy, born in Neishapour
1150	Sufi poet Sana'i dies. His famous book *The Garden of The Truth* had major influence on Rumi. He developed genre of Persian religious, as opposed to courtly, poetry in which Rumi wrote.

1210–1212   Baha al-Din moves family to cultural center of
             Samarqand, also located in Khorosan

1216–1221   Baha al-Din leaves Khorosan altogether, bringing
             disciples and members of extended family with
             him, including his wife Mo'mene Khatun and
             their sons, Rumi and Ala al-Din. Exact date of
             departure is hard to fix, but many scholars place it
             in 1217, when Rumi was ten years old.

1217–1222   Baha al-Din begins period of wandering through
             medieval Middle East. Entourage probably stops
             first in Baghdad; then makes pilgrimage to
             Mecca. By legend there is a stay in Neishapour,
             where Rumi allegedly met Sufi writer Attar.
             Pilgrimage is followed by stays of indefinite
             length in Damascus and Malatya, and period of
             several years in which family remains in town of
             Aqshahr, where it enjoys favor of local princess.

1220–1224   Sometime during this period family settles in town
             of Larende in Anatolia, or modern Turkey. Rumi is
             now a young man. During this period he experi-
             ences the death of his mother and his own marriage
             to Gowhar Khatun. His sons, Ala al-Din and Sultan
             Valad, are born in Larende.

1229   Baha al-Din moves family to Konya; receives good
             teaching position in local madrase. Many other
             refugees from Khorosan also attracted to Anatolia
             because of tolerant atmosphere under Seljuk rule.

1212	Khwarasmshah overtakes Samarqand in violent siege in which many men are killed and many women raped. Rumi was about five years old and living in Samarqand at the time. Children's Crusade
1221	Mongol army overtakes Balkh and other cities of Khorosan. Baha al-Din and family most likely had left area much earlier.
1225	Third reissue of Magna Carta in definitive form
1225-1235	Distinguished Andalusian Sufi mystic Mohyi al-Din Ibn Arabi moves to Syria, where he attracts large following. Both Rumi and Shams may have heard him speak during this period. Despite his influence, Shams considered him phony.
1227	Death of St. Francis of Assissi, Christian mystic to whom Rumi often is compared Ghenghis Khan dies; three sons divide empire
1228	Sixth Crusade, led by Emperor Frederick II
1229	Frederick II, crowned King of Jerusalem, signs treaty with the Sultan of Egypt

1231	Baha al-Din passes away
1232	Baha al-Din's old teacher Sayyed Borhan al-Din Mohaqqeq turns up in Konya, unaware of Baha's death; oversees final portion of Rumis' education
1232–1240	Rumi spends much time at elite seminaries in Syria, perfecting his knowledge of Islam. Begins to delve into his late father's diaries and to study mysticism. During stays in Syria, he is separated from wife and children for long stretches of time.
1239–1244	Rumi resettles in Konya for good, taking up his father's old post at madrase. During this period, prior to his poetic outpouring, he earns reputation as legal thinker, outstanding speaker and restorer of Islam. First wife Gowhar Khatun passes away; remarries and with second wife, Kerra Khatun, has son and daughter.
1244	Nov. 29: Shams al-Din of Tabriz arrives in Konya; Rumi is immediately captivated by Shams, but many of his disciples plot against Shams, some wishing to drive him out of town
1245	Mar. 11: Shams leaves Konya for Syria; Rumi is disconsolate
Early 1247	Sultan Valad escorts Shams back to Konya, where dervish receives a hero's welcome
Mid-1247	Rumi overjoyed by Shams' return; some disciples break promises and resume plot against dervish
Late 1247	Shams disappears. Rumi never sees him again. Some scholars believe he was murdered, possibly by Rumi's son Ala al-Din. Others believe he returned to Syria or began another period of wandering.
1248–1249	Rumi makes at least two unsuccessful trips to Syria, to search for Shams; begins writing many of his "ghazals," or shorter verses
1250	Rumi finally reconciles himself to fact that he will never see Shams again; selects a goldsmith, Salah al-Din, as his new Beloved, again sparking jeal-

1237   Seljuk leader Ghiyasoddin Keykhosrow ascends
         throne; reign is ineffectual and marred by political
         insurgency

1242   Mongols invade Anatolia, but do not overtake
         Konya in violent manner; some allege Rumi's
         presence spared town. Seljuk leader Ghiyasoddin
         Keykhosrow is allowed to remain as figurehead,
         but his power is limited.

1245   Ghiyasoddin Keykhosrow dies, leaving three sons
         who feud among themselves; in time all three
         succumb to their enemies

ousy and criticism among disciples

1258   Salah al-Din passes away; Hosam al-Din, a long-time friend of Rumi's, is chosen as successor

1261–1264   Rumi begins composing the *Mathnawi*

1273   Dec. 17: Rumi dies, by legend at sunset; his second wife Kerra Khatun is to outlive him by 19 years

1258	Mongols take Baghdad and overthrow caliphate
1260	First mastersinger school (Mainz)
1274	A year after Rumi's death, Egyptian Baibars topple Mu'in al-Din, the Mongol vassal of Anatolia. The vassal, a close friend of poet, spared Konya from worst aggressions of the Mongols.
1278	Hosam al-Din, the last of Rumis' beloved friends, dies
Invention of the glass mirror
1284	Sultan Valad begins organizing the Mevlevi Order
1301	Sultan Valad passes away at age 84
Early 15 C.	Ottoman sultans begin to exert control over Mevlevi Order, taking away much of its independent character, but enabling its music, calligraphy and poetry to spread throughout much of world
1809	Selim III, Ottomon Sultan, composer and member of Mevlevi Order, dies
1925	Kemal Ataturk declares Sufism illegal in Turkey. Rumi's shrine becomes state-run museum for benefit of tourists. Sufis endure persecution.
1953	Turkish government permits Mevlevi Order to perform sama under supervised conditions, chiefly for tourists
1990	Kabir Helminski initiated as Mevlevi sheikh; first American to have this honor

NOTES

CHAPTER 1: THE POET OF LOVE AND TUMULT

1. Nicholson, *The Mathnawi, Books I and II*, p. 67.
2. Schimmel, *The Triumphal Sun*, p. 13.
3. Star, *Rumi: In the Arms of the Beloved*, p. 12
4. Keshavartz, *Reading Mystical Lyric; The Case of Jalal al-Din Rumi*, p. 7.

CHAPTER 2: A HARSH CHILDHOOD OF FEW FACTS

1. Arberry, *The Discourses of Rumi*, p. 173.
2. Schimmel, *The Triumphal Sun*, p. 16.

CHAPTER 3: A KING WITH NO DOMINION

1. Lewis, *Rumi, Past and Present, East and West*, p. 52.
2. Ibid., p. 88.
3. Ibid., p. 82.
4. Ibid., p. 41.

CHAPTER 4 THE NEVER-ENDING JOURNEY

1. Nicholson, *The Mathnawi, Books V and VI*, p. 309.

Chapter 5: Konya, At Long Last

1. Nicholson, *The Mathnawi, Books III and IV*, p. 82.
2. Lewis, Rumi, Past and Present, East and West, p. 100.
3. Ibid., p. 102.
4. de Vitray-Meyerovitch, *Rumi and Sufism*, p. 38.
5. Arberry, *The Discourses of Rumi*, p. 98.
6. Nicholson, *Rumi: Poet and Mystic*, p. 45.

Chapter 6: Friend to Kings and Ruffians

1. Nicholson, *The Mathnawi, Books I and II*, p. 81.
2. Arberry, *The Discourses of Rumi*, p. 17.
3. Iqbal, Afzal, *The Life & Work of Jalaluddin Rumi*, p. 105.
4. Lewis, *Rumi, Past and Present, East and West*,
   p. 122.
5. Ibid., p. 320.
6. Iqbal, Afzal, *The Life and Work of Jalaluddin Rumi*, p. 105.

Chapter 7: A Love So Divine

1. Nicholson, *The Mathnawi, Books I and II*, p. 75.
2. Lewis, *Rumi, Past and Present, East and West*, p. 142.
3. Ibid., p. 142.
4. Ibid., p. 150.
5. Ibid., p. 143.
6. Ibid., p. 146.
7. Ibid., p. 154.
8. Ibid., p. 154.
9. Iqbal, Afzal, *The Life & Workof Jalaluddin Rumi*, p. 114.
10. Lewis, *Rumi, Past and Present, East and West*, p. 155.
11. Ibid., p. 155.
12. Ibid., p. 159.
13. Ibid., p. 164.

14. Iqbal, *The Life & Work of Jalaluddin Rumi*, p. 115.
15. Lewis, *Rumi, Past and Present, East and West*, p. 144.
16. Cowan, *Rumi's Divan of Shams of Tabriz* pp. 17–18.
17. Lewis, *Rumi, Past and Present, East and West*, p. 162.

CHAPTER 8: LIFE AFTER LOVE: THE DEPARTURE OF SHAMS

1. Cowan, *Rumi's Divan of Shams of Tabriz*, p. 114.
2. Lewis, *Rumi, Past and Present, East and West*,
   p. 181.
3. Cowan, *Rumi's Divan of Shams of Tabriz*, p. 63.
4. Nicholson, *The Mathnawi, Books III and IV*, p. 174.
5. Lewis, *Rumi, Past and Present, East and West*,
   p. 164.
6. Cowan, *Rumi's Divan of Shams of Tabriz*, p. 127.
7. Ibid., p. 10.

CHAPTER 9: MAD FOR MUSIC

1. Nicholson, *The Mathnawi, Books III and IV*, p. 33.
2. Cowan, *Rumi's Divan of Shams of Tabriz*, p. 19.
3. Keshavarz, *Reading Mystical Lyric, the Case of Jalal al-Din Rumi*, p. 112.
4. Lewis, *Rumi, Past and Present, East and West*, p. 193.
5. Ibid, p. 183.
6. Cowan, *Rumi's Divan of Shams of Tabriz*, p. 85.
7. Ibid, p. 107.
8. Schimmel, *The Triumphal Sun*, p. 26.
9. Ibid, p. 27.
10. Nicholson, *The Mathnawi, Books I and II*, p. 5.
11. Ibid., p. IV.
12. Ibid, p. 3.

Chapter 10: The Most Digressive Story Ever Told

1. Nicholson, *The Mathnawi, Books III and IV*, p. 236.
2. Ibid.
3. Lewis, *Rumi, Past and Present, East and West*, p. 399.
4. Nicholson, *The Mathnawi, Books I and II*, p. XIV.
5. Ibid.
6. Nicholson, *The Mathnawi, Books III and IV*, p. 238.
7. Schimmel, *The Triumphal Sun*, p. 49.
8. Nicholson, *The Mathnawi, Books III and IV*, p. 271.

Chapter 11: Death Dervish-Style

1. Cowan, *Rumi's Divan of Shams of Tabriz*, pp. 73–74
2. Nicholson, *The Mathnawi, Books V and VI*, p. 529.
3. Ibid.
4. Ibid.
5. Iqbal, *The Life & Times of Jalaluddin Rumi*, p. 136.
6. Nicholson, *The Mathnawi, Books V and VI*, p. 302.
7. Lewis, *Rumi, Past and Present, East and West*, p. 223.

BIBLIOGRAPHY

al-Ghazzali, Abu Hamid Mohammad. *The Alchemy of Happiness*, Armonk, New York: M. E. Sharpe Inc., 1991.

Arberry, A.J. *Discourses of Rumi*, Surrey: Curzon Press Ltd, 1961.

———. *Tales from the Masnavi*, Surrey, Curzon Press Ltd, 1961.

———. *Mystical Poems of Rumi, First Selection*, Poems 1-200, Chicago: University of Chicago Press, 1968.

Attar, Farid ud-Din. *The Conference of the Birds*, London: Penguin Books, 1984.

Bakhtiar, Laleh. *Sufi Expressions of the Mystic Quest*, London: Thames and Hudson Press, 1976.

Barks, Coleman with John Moyne. *The Essential Rumi*, San Francisco: HarperSanFrancisco, 1995.

———. *Rumi—We are Three, New Rumi Translations*, Athens, Georgia: Maypop Books, 1987.

Cowan, James. *Rumi's Divan of Shams of Tabriz*, Rockport, Mass: Element Classics of World Spirituality, 1997.

de Vitray-Meyerovitch, Eva, *Rumi and Sufism*, Sausalito, California: Post-Apollo Press, 1987.

Ernst, Carl. *Teaching Sufism*, Boston: Shambhala Press, 1999.

———. *Sufism, an Essential Introduction*, Boston: Shambhala Press, 1997.

Helminski, Camille and Kabir. *Rumi Daylight: A Daybook of Spiritual Guidance*, Boston: Shambhala Press, 1999.

Hillenbrand, Carole. *The Crusades, Islamic Perspectives*, Edinburgh: Edinburgh University Press, 1999.

Iqbal, Afzal, *The Life and Work of Jalaluddin Rumi*, London: The Octagon Press, 1956.

Farhadi, A. G. Ravan. *Abdullah Ansari of Herat, An Early Sufi Master*, Surrey: Curzon Press Ltd, 1996.

Keshavarz, Fatemeh. *Reading Mystical Lyre; The Case of Jalal al-Din Rumi*, Colombia, South Carolina: University of South Carolina Press, 1998.

Lewis, Franklin. *Rumi, Past and Present, East and West; The Life, Teachings and Poetry of Jalal al-Din Rumi*, Oxford, England: Oneworld Publications, 2000.

Lewisohn, Leonard. *The Heritage of Sufism; Classical Persian Sufism from its Origins to Rumi*, Oxford, England: Oneworld Publications, 1999.

Nicholson, Reynold A. *The Mathnawi of Jalalu'din Rumi, Books I and II*, Cambridge, England: E.J.W. Gibb Memorial Trust, 1926.

———. *The Mathnawi of Jalalu'din Rumi, Books III and IV*, Cambridge, England: E.J.W. Gibb Memorial Trust, 1926.

———. *The Mathnawi of Jalalu'din Rumi, Books V and VI*, Cambridge, England: E.J.W. Gibb Memorial Trust, 1926.

———. *Rumi: Poet & Mystic*, E.J.W. Gibb Memorial Trust, 1926.

Schimmel, Annemarie. *The Triumphal Sun: A Study of the Works of Jalaluddin Rumi*, Albany, New York: State University of New York Press, 1993.

Shah, Indries. *The Sufis*, New York: Doubleday, 1964.

Star, Jonathan. *Rumi: In the Arms of the Beloved*, New York: Penguin Putnam Inc., 1997.

Thackston, W. M. *Signs of the Unsees; the Discourses of Jalaluddin Rumi*, Boston: Shambhala Press, 1999.

Trimingham, J. Spencer. *The Sufi Orders of Islam*, Oxford: Oxford University Press, 1971.

INDEX